Life into Art

*L*ife into *A*rt

Conversations with
Seven Contemporary Biographers

Gail Porter Mandell

The University of Arkansas Press
Fayetteville   London   1991

95 94 93 92 91   5 4 3 2 1

*This book was designed by Ch. H. Russell
using the Sabon typeface.*

The paper used in this publication meets the minimum requirements
of the American National Standard for Permanence of Paper for
Printed Library Materials Z39.48-1984. ⬡

Library of Congress Cataloging-in-Publication Data

Mandell, Gail Porter 1940–
    Life into Art: conversations with seven contemporary biographers
/ Gail Porter Mandell.
            p.   cm.
    Includes bibliographical references.
    ISBN 1–55728–180–7 (alk. paper).
    1. Biography (as a literary form)   2. Biographers—Interviews.
I. Title.
CT21.M25   1991
808'.06692—dc20

                                                90-36491
                                                    CIP

For
Penny Brooke Jameson

Acknowledgments

Augusta Donovan Foley, my maternal grandmother, planted the seed of this book many years ago, in the long afternoons of my childhood when, in answer to my incessant questions and out of her own compulsion, she told me the life stories of relatives and family friends. What a storyteller she was—the best I have ever known—with her sure sense of the drama of everyday life and its origin in human character. Thanks to her, I experienced early on the pleasures of biography and autobiography.

The idea of discussing the art of biography with contemporary biographers came to me many years later. It began as part of a year-long study of biography funded jointly by Saint Mary's College, Notre Dame, Indiana, where I teach among others a course on biography called "Lives and Times," and by the Lilly Endowment, Incorporated, of Indianapolis, Indiana. Special thanks go to President William A. Hickey and Dean Dorothy M. Feigl of Saint Mary's and to William C. Bonifield, Vice President for Education at the Endowment, for their generous support. I would also like to thank Colin Bull, William H. Harris, William A. Kinnison, and Mary-Linda Merriam, who reviewed the project for the Lilly Endowment and offered many helpful suggestions for its completion.

Of course, the project itself and the book that has resulted from it would have been impossible without the cooperation of the seven individuals who agreed to these conversations. At no slight inconvenience to themselves and often their families, they made time in their busy schedules to meet with me and, later, to read and comment upon my transcription of our interview. Several opened their homes to me, fed me, and otherwise looked after me. Many went out of their way to meet me at times and places convenient for me. The magnitude of their individual and collective generosity stunned me, and their warm encouragement for this undertaking moved me greatly. In particular, Michael Mott, who read and recommended my proposal to Lilly, and Paul Mariani, who at a crucial stage encouraged me to expand the project, deserve special acknowledgment. To them and to Edwin McClellan, Arnold Rampersad, Phyllis Rose, Jonathan Spence, and Elisabeth Young-Bruehl, my deepest gratitude.

Heartfelt thanks also go to my students, past and present, whose interest in and questions about biography have inspired my own and to my friends and colleagues Ann Loux; Bruno Schlesinger; Linnea Vacca; Elena Malits, C.S.C.; Jean Klene, C.S.C.; John Matthias; Tom Bonnell; John Shinners; and Julie Long, all of whom took a lively interest in the project and offered invaluable help or advice at critical stages. Above all, I would like to thank Penny Jameson, with whom I carried on a running conversation about biography, these interviews, and everything else important in my life. Her contributions have been invaluable and her friendship of twenty years, along with that of her husband, Ken, indispensable and irreplaceable.

During the two years and more of this project, my husband, Daniel, has, with characteristic good humor, kindness, and patience, minimized every difficulty. His love and unqualified support and that of my family—my mother and stepfather, Genevieve and Benjamin Henneman; my father, Howard Porter; my mother-in-law, Elizabeth Mandell—make my work possible.

Nor can I fail to thank those at the University of Arkansas Press whose exceptional competence and courtesy have made the publication of this book a happy experience. In particular, I thank Deborah Navas and Debbie Bowen, who have been most careful and considerate editors.

Contents

Introduction

Fifty years ago, Virginia Woolf called biography a "young art." Compared with the creative genius displayed in the genres of poetry and fiction, she found biography lacking. Was that the fault of the form or of its practitioners? Woolf left that implicit question for future resolution. Unable to name the biographer "whose art is subtle and bold enough to present that queer amalgamation of dream and reality," which in her opinion biography requires, she concluded, "His method still remains to be discovered."[1]

Anyone who surveys the shelves of any bookstore knows that biography is currently a booming business. Hundreds of new titles in the genre appear annually in English alone. Their contents span a broad spectrum, from individual lives of the famous and infamous, alive and dead, to social biographies of classes of people from the very rich to the very poor. Today it seems that no life, whether of illiterate sharecropper or mass murderer, is too obscure or ignominious to tell.

Along with autobiography, also a burgeoning form in Western culture, biography today is experiencing what has been called a "golden age." Biography and autobiography suit the temper of our individualistic age, just as drama suited the spirit of the Elizabethan age and the many-volumed

1

novel satisfied Victorian taste. With so many now practicing the art of biography, it seems a propitious time to sample the opinion of biographers themselves on the state of the art. What are their methods and aims? What are their insights into this developing genre?

Over the past few years, I talked with seven contemporary but quite different biographers in circumstances described in the introduction to each conversation. They represent a range of biographical writing. Paul Mariani and Arnold Rampersad write in what has become the traditional mode of literary biography, in which the biographer examines in detail the relation of a writer's art to his life. Michael Mott also writes in this mode, although his subject, who also produced texts, is not strictly speaking a literary figure. The work of Phyllis Rose includes numerous types of biography (based on texts in most cases, but not all) and a wide range of subjects (often literary figures, but not always), united by her quest for the psychological underpinnings of the lives she tells—what she calls the "personal mythologies" of her subjects. Edwin McClellan writes in a belletristic, Western mode about a Japanese woman and her family, using as his source a Japanese biographical text that is a classic in that country. Experimental and thus not easily classifiable, the work of Jonathan Spence starts from various types of texts—not necessarily written by his subjects. From as few as six lines in one instance, he recreates the worlds and minds of men and women somehow connected with his field of Chinese history. Finally, Elisabeth Young-Bruehl characterizes her particular approach as "psychobiography," which she defines as biography that is "psychologically oriented and guided by psychological theory."

Following the opinion of biographer Justin Kaplan that a strong case can be made for "enlarging the term 'literary biography' to include books that have literary qualities and not necessarily literary subjects,"[2] I chose to interview biographers who take a literary approach, broadly defined, to their material. Each of these biographers consciously aspires to create literature: that is, to create works of art distinguished by beauty of form and expression. Not content with craftsmanship, they strive to accomplish what Woolf maintained the great biographer must do; that is, "weld . . . into one seamless whole" the "granite-like solidity" of truth and the "rainbow-like intangibility" of personality. No less than the historian, they desire to ascertain the facts of the lives of their subjects, but like the novelist, they also aim to create through language the illusion of life. In Woolf's terms, they struggle to bring a young art to maturity.

These biographers tend to be "literary" in yet another sense. All work primarily from texts written by (or in a few cases about) their subjects; in most instances, these are literary texts. As a rule, they focus on the minds or psyches of their subjects as opposed to their deeds. The text serves as the biographer's way into the minds, and through the minds into the lives and worlds of his or her subjects. This route may be contrasted with that of the more historically oriented biographer—sometimes referred to as the "chronicler"—who, although using texts perhaps, scrutinizes actions or events, of which human personality explains only a part. It also differs from the approach of the so-called "critical biographer," who uses the life of the subject to illuminate the work, rather than vice versa.

The seven interviewed here, including historians McClellan and Spence, resemble the essayist more than the archivist. All stress that biographers must hold themselves to high standards of verification and pride themselves on the thoroughness of their research; nevertheless, whether explicitly or implicitly, they define biography as "storytelling."

The work of these biographers suggests that those who depend upon literary texts, as these biographers do, share important similarities (however great their differences may be in other respects) that distinguish them from biographers

3

who base the lives they tell on different types of material. Most important, they assume that the written text reveals the psyche of the one who wrote it, so that all literature becomes in essence autobiography. The biographer becomes in varying degrees a psychoanalyst, reconstructing the story of the self from psychic correspondences.

Furthermore, literary biographers relate to their readers differently from those whose sources are more disparate or less ambiguous. In effect, the biographer who works from texts offers his or her interpretation as just that—one way of construing a reality which acts as a sign of a still more complex reality, that of the subject him or herself. For this reason, Rampersad calls biographical writing an "art of approximation." Literary biography, unlike historical biography, allows readers to enter into the act of interpretation by drawing their own opinions about the text, which serves as source material. In the case of the historical biographer, the act of interpretation often remains veiled, concealed by a patina of fact.

Within this still broad category of literary biography, I selected biographers who, while writing in English, represent a cross section of cultures, class, race, and gender. In some cases, this diversity is represented not only by the biographers themselves but also by their subjects. In the interviews, the biographers reflected upon the significance of these differences upon their work. Rose and Young-Bruehl, for example, discussed the impact of gender on both their research and writing. Mariani spoke about how his working-class background affected his choice of biographical subjects and his view of the literary canon. Rampersad considered race as it has influenced his own work and that of his subject, Langston Hughes. Both McClellan and Spence brought up the benefits and difficulties of bridging cultures with biography. Such considerations highlight some of the characteristic features of biography in the twentieth century.

4

In her essay "Fact and Fiction in Biography," Rose has written: "Biography is still shaking off assumptions about fit subjects closer to those of classical tragedy, which dealt only with royalty and heroes, although, to satisfy our secular sense of the sacred, it has traditionally added artists and writers. In biography, the bourgeois-democratic revolution is just beginning."[3] In their choice of subjects, several of these biographers further that sense of revolution, most notably Spence, who writes about an insignificant Chinese peasant woman, and McClellan, who focuses on an obscure Japanese woman. Others present an aspect of their subject's experience previously ignored by other biographers—as Rampersad does, for example, in his portrait of life in the black community to which Langston Hughes belonged. Similarly, Rose and Young-Bruehl regard themselves as exploring areas of experience of their female subjects that male biographers have missed. As these writers demonstrate, biographers today are engaged in the task of defining what it means to be human, factoring in gender, class, and race in a way rarely attempted in the past.

As both their work and their personalities confirm, this is a diverse group of writers who represent a wide spectrum of biographical writing. They illustrate the extremes that labels such as "literary biography" and "biography of the mind" encompass. To emphasize this breadth, I have positioned the interviews to approximate the range of biographical writing today. The collection begins with those literary biographers who identify with a biographical tradition that originated with Samuel Johnson and James Boswell; it ends with those who consciously push at accepted limits of the form. In this way, the reader can adopt an increasingly radical perspective on biographical form and content. At the same time, hearing these different voices in concert, one discerns more readily the many common strains in such diversity.

I allowed these conversations to flow freely, choosing not to focus them on a central issue or theme, so that the distinctive

5

sensibility of each biographer might emerge. I did, however, bring up many of the same questions in each interview: questions such as the biographer's definition of "biography," the nature of biography today, the biographer's relation to his or her subject, and the biographer's own process of writing biography. Consequently, the reader will find recurring themes in the collection.

In editing the conversations, which I first transcribed verbatim from tape, I stayed as close to the original as clarity and coherence allowed. Most of the changes I made were to eliminate the repetition and diffuseness inevitable in conversation. I then sent a copy of the interview to each biographer for further editing, with queries about unclear sections. In every case, the biographer made few and relatively minor changes, usually recommending that parts be cut rather than altered.

What did I conclude about contemporary biography after interviewing these seven individuals? First of all, the biographers with whom I spoke would wholeheartedly agree with Virginia Woolf's assessment that "the new biography" of this century is different from that of earlier periods. As Young-Bruehl put it in her interview, "Biography is a genre whose modern origins are in the 1920s. Of course, it has big antecedents, say in the eighteenth century, and it has its Plutarch, but it's basically a twentieth-century phenomenon. It is a particular cultural effervescence and to understand why this should be so and why the fascination should be so is one of the most interesting questions to ask yourself as you think about this genre as a genre."

Indeed, I often asked myself, and those I interviewed, that question. The most obvious answer to emerge from the biographers themselves is the vital connection between psychology and biography today. Not only Young-Bruehl, who has committed herself to a psychological approach in her work, but all those interviewed emphasized the impact on their art of twentieth-century psychological thought, most often that of Freud. Like Rampersad, many admitted that they have not gone deeply into psychological theory; nevertheless, they stressed their desire to explore the inner lives of their subjects. As Spence defined it in his interview, the enterprise of the contemporary biographer is "trying to enter somebody else's mind."

The illumination of the inner life of the subject is a peculiarly contemporary aim of biography, indebted ultimately to psychoanalytic theory. So is the use of a text as entrée into the subjective world of its author. The presumption is that such texts began as thoughts or images that reveal essential features of the individual human psyche. Through them, the biographer aims to present the subject as he or she might know him or herself, using the written word as the link between inner and outer realities.

A further psychological perspective includes the biographer's search for self-understanding through identification with the subject. The biographer may go so far as to envy and wish to appropriate certain qualities of the subject. Ultimately, every biography would seem to have something in it of the biographer's own life.

McClellan offers a subtle variation in this regard. Basing his work on an early twentieth-century Japanese biography, he respects the reticence of his source, Mori Ōgai, whose approach he described as "very different from that of contemporary Western biographers who try to reveal the inner lives of their subjects." Although he sympathizes with Ōgai's sense of decorum, McClellan nevertheless described as fundamental to his own biography a desire to enter the mind not of his and Ōgai's shared subjects but of Ōgai himself, whose work he has translated and adapted to his own purposes.

These biographers, then, take an essentially different point of view in their work from that of earlier ages. They view their subjects and the lives of their subjects from within rather than without. This often leads to an identification with the subject so intense that, as Rose illustrates in the case of her narration of Virginia Woolf's suicide, it can threaten the biographer herself. The biographer's artistic challenge becomes achieving a proper distance from the subject through tone and point of view.

Not surprisingly, these biographers feel the tension between their contemporary need to present the subject from within and an expectation of detachment and impartiality on the part of some readers, which stems from a more traditional model of biography. One after another confessed in these conversations, some apologetically and others defiantly, that reviewers have accused them of writing "uncritically" of their subjects, an accusation that has clearly drawn blood. This tension, much remarked upon in the literature about the genre, has to some extent always characterized biography; modern practice has simply exacerbated it. In fact, the contemporary biographers' intimacy with their subjects would seem to derive from and be essential to their biographical approach and may very well be incompatible with a more distanced view.

Nevertheless, "the biographer is an artist upon oath," as Desmond McCarthy put it in a much-quoted remark. In other words, however inventive he or she may be, the biographer must first tell the truth in a way no writer of fiction is obliged to do, as these seven writers individually emphasized in their conversations. Weaving a story out of facts, the biographer shares with the scientist a basic concern with objectivity and accuracy—a concern that may explain something of the appeal of biography in our scientific age. Ironically, by contributing to the transformation of the idea of the self, which lies at the core of biography, the sciences (psychology among them) can be said to have transformed biography in the modern age to fit its specifications.

Paradoxically, perhaps, these conversations reveal that along with the identification of author with subject goes the sense that the "real" person can never be recaptured. The dual assumption seems to be that, on the one hand, no one can ever penetrate the mystery of another (a position that recalls William James's claim that "the greatest breach in nature is the breach between two minds") and, on the other, that the biographer can in fact know certain things about the subject better than the subject him or herself could (no doubt another Freudian legacy). Consequently, the biographer becomes both psychoanalyst and confessor.

Because of the biographer's power of interpretation, these writers stress the necessity of artistic and ethical integrity. They regard the subject as particularly vulnerable; even a "victim," as one of these biographers put it. All seem wary of the difficulties of knowing both the self and others, and regard the telling of lives as an almost sacred task.

Yet, surprisingly, none wants to be thought of, first and foremost, as a biographer. This attitude suggests that today, as in Woolf's day, biography does not yet have a secure place among the creative arts. To tell a life is a sacred task because life itself is regarded as sacred, not because biography is an elevated art form—as is poetry, for example.

The mixed feelings about biography of those interviewed also suggest, and may in part result from, the ambiguous role of biography in the academy, with which all of these particular biographers are associated. As Rampersad pointed out, many biographies originate in the academic world, where publishing is paramount. Even so, biographies are rarely included on course syllabi; as a genre, biography has not yet become a subject that is regularly taught in departments of literature or history.

Nor is biography fully accepted as an appropriate scholarly enterprise. Several of these biographers remarked upon the marginal nature of their work. Most, however, regard biography as a way of revitalizing scholarship and the academy. Spence, for example, turned to biography as a way of experimenting with the form of historical writing. Others regard biography as a way to revitalize and personalize their scholarly research and writing. With some irony,

Mariani commented on the significant effect biography in fact has on what is taught in the academy, from which works of biography are as a rule excluded.

Be that as it may, these biographers agree that their primary purpose must be to tell the life, not criticize the work of the subject. They reject the idea that the main purpose of literary biography is literary criticism. Instead, as mentioned earlier, they insist that biography should be regarded primarily as "storytelling." Exactly what do they mean, and how does this type of storytelling either resemble or differ from other forms of narration?

The stories these writers tell are obviously "true" stories as opposed to fictional ones, although all expressed some doubt about how close to the truth of a life anyone, the subject included, can come. Taking as their reference point the reality of a life, biography and autobiography would seem to be closely related forms of storytelling. In their interviews, however, both Rampersad and Mott pointed out that biography significantly differs from autobiography in its relation to fact. Being frankly subjective, the latter is free to include impressions and depend upon memory alone in a way that biography cannot.

Rose has written that biographers are unnecessarily intimidated by both "an Anglo-American respect for fact which makes [them] timid and a naiveté about the nature of fact."[4] While biography and fiction are clearly distinct genres, she emphasizes that biographers have successfully adopted certain fictional techniques, especially those relating to point of view and shift of chronology. Most of these biographers look to fiction (indeed, several write fiction as well as biography) to confirm their experiments with biographical form.

The writing of Jonathan Spence demonstrates how one need not sacrifice inventive narration for historical accuracy. Consider his *Memory Palace of Matteo Ricci,* in which Spence organizes the facts of the life of a sixteenth-century

Jesuit missionary to China around certain symbols and images important to his subject. The reader consequently finds the account of Ricci's death midway through the book, and details of his boyhood at its conclusion.

As Spence's work demonstrates, the chronological arrangement of a life history, although customary, is not essential to biography, even if it is essential to the living of a life. His work provokes the realization that the biographer conventionally assumes a narrative stance that implies that both author and reader are accompanying the subject as he or she moves through time. By taking the reader into the mind—in particular, the memory—of his subject, Spence demonstrates the possibility of other narrative stances.

In *Matteo Ricci*—as in *Emperor of China,* a montage of seventeenth-century Emperor K'ang-hsi's autobiographical writings, and *Death of Woman Wang,* the story of a murder of a seventeenth-century Chinese peasant woman by her husband—author and reader enter the mental processes of the subject as the subject experiences, thinks about, and remembers life. The point of entry is in each case a particular text, usually written by the subject. Instead of organizing around external events, the author patterns material according to the way in which the mind, and in particular the memory, works—by association and according to both pervasive cultural and unique psychic patterns. Thus, chronology becomes one way among many through which the subject—and the biographer—organizes experience. In Spence's work, the chronology of a life reveals itself to be a mental abstraction, while physical sensation and mental images become as primary as time is in most biographies. Spence's book invites the thought that as conventions change, achronological biographies may become as common as achronological novels now are.

Although few biographers depart as radically from conventional form as Spence does, others whom I interviewed

11

consistently described the form of their books as "organic," that is, growing out of the nature of their material. An apparent—but not real—exception to this organic approach to form is that of McClellan in *Woman in the Crested Kimono*. Because he based his work on that of another biographer, he adopted perforce a predetermined form. Nevertheless, in retelling Mori Ōgai's story of Shibue Chūsai, a nineteenth-century doctor and scholar, he radically alters its form through what amounts to a radical shift in perspective. What was an extended narrative of the life of a man and his family becomes in McClellan's hands a subtly layered narrative about narration. At the heart of the slender book is now Shibue Io, Chūsai's fourth wife, whose story is the consequence of tales told by her son Tamotsu (many of which presumably originated with Io herself), retold by Ōgai, and finally repeated by McClellan, who serves as translator, interpreter, and ultimate narrator. Their fascination with Io unites all three narrators, serving as McClellan's way into the mind of his source, Ōgai, as well as the life of their shared subject, Io.

By using first-person narration to discuss both Ōgai's and Tamotsu's presentation of their shared material, McClellan jolts the reader into a sophisticated awareness of authorial presence. Through the figure of Ōgai, McClellan introduces the biographer as overt intermediary; he himself then serves as a visible model of the biographer at work, investigating, interpreting, and assimilating his sources. In its experimentation with point of view, this work suggests that although narrative detachment may be a widely accepted convention of contemporary biography, neither scholarship nor elegance of style requires it. Ironically, the frankness of McClellan's presence in his text serves to distance him, and his reader, from Io herself—detachment that McClellan regards as not inappropriate to his subject.

Both Spence and McClellan exist at the "far reaches" of biography. Indeed, not only reviewers but also they themselves have trouble classifying their work, although it comes as close to being biography as anything else. In *Parallel Lives*, Rose also pushes at the present limits of the genre, not in the content of the biographies included in the book but, as she says, in her arrangement of them. As does Plutarch, whose title she wittily adapts to her purposes, Rose presses biography into the service of an idea, in this case about modern marriage. She does so by juxtaposing the lives of five Victorian couples, for which she provides a political framework, compelling the reader to reinterpret the lives in reference to a larger context. In this instance, biography renews its ancient didactic purpose in a contemporary, altogether fresh way.

Not only do the conversations recorded in the following pages reveal a predilection of those interviewed for organic form but also for what might be called "organic style." All those interviewed betrayed a concern that the language in which a life is told be appropriate to the spirit of that life. Some went so far as to insist that the biography of a writer must reflect the aesthetic qualities of the work of the subject. For example, in the language of her biographies of Hannah Arendt and Anna Freud, Young-Bruehl consciously emulated the literary styles of her subjects. Going a step beyond, McClellan defined sensitivity to the language in which his text is written as a prerequisite to understanding the lives and culture depicted in his biography. In the work of these biographers, language itself becomes a bridge that links author, subject, and reader.

It is a commonplace that biography as a genre resists systematic study because of its hybrid nature. But as a rule, those who have practiced the art have had most to say about it: writers like Samuel Johnson in the eighteenth century; John Gibson Lockhart and Thomas Carlyle in the nineteenth; and Virginia Woolf, André Maurois, Sir Nigel Nicholson, and Leon Edel in the twentieth. Like their antecedents, the seven biographers represented here have thought deeply and critically about their art. Many deplore the lack of critical acumen about biography on the part of critics and general readers alike. As he has written in "Reassembling the Dust," Mariani finds this a "curious phenomenon" in an age that "prides itself on the attention it has given to the critical act."[5] Young-Bruehl expressed a similar idea in her interview: "There's no cultivated readership for biography, because people are only reading for the life story. If you asked most people, 'Well, what kinds of things make a good biography?' you would draw a blank." The conversations that follow should do much to enhance the ability of general readers and critics alike to read the work of these biographers, and of others like them, with the perspicacity it so richly deserves!

Notes

1. Virginia Woolf, "The Art of Biography" and "The New Biography" from *Collected Essays,* Volume 4 (New York: Harcourt, Brace and World, 1925, reprinted 1967), 221–33.

2. quoted in Stephen B. Oates, ed., *Biography as High Adventure: Life-Writers on Their Art* (Amherst: University of Massachusetts Press, 1986), xi.

3. Phyllis Rose, "Fact and Fiction in Biography," collected in *Writing of Women: Essays in a Renaissance* (Middletown: Wesleyan University Press, 1985), 75.

4. Rose, 81.

5. in Oates, ed., 104.

Conversation with

Paul Mariani

When they learned of my intention to interview contemporary biographers, several people independently of each other encouraged me to contact Paul Mariani. "His biography of William Carlos Williams is first-rate," one of them said, "and besides, he's a really decent man." So I plunged into *William Carlos Williams: A New World Naked,* and, as I was told I would, thoroughly enjoyed myself. I then read with delight his collections of poetry: *Timing Devices, Crossing Cocytus,* and *Prime Mover,* and ended by surveying a collection of his essays, *A Usable Past,* and several critical works: *A Commentary on the Complete Poems of Gerard Manley Hopkins* and *William Carlos Williams: The Poet and His Critics.* Moreover, I learned, he was just finishing a biography of the poet John Berryman. Would Mariani be too busy to see me? I wondered as I sent off a letter asking for an interview.

Mariani's response was an immediate telephone call. His rich, rapid voice, definitely East Coast, filled the line. His answer: "Let's do it!"

We met at a restaurant near the football stadium at the University of Massachusetts at Amherst, where Mariani is a professor in the department of English. A big man, he might plausibly have played linebacker earlier in life. A few minutes late for our meeting, he explained that he had just returned from an unexpected trip to Albany. A friend in his late forties, about Mariani's age and also a writer, had been buried that morning—dead of a heart attack. Driving back, Mariani narrowly missed an accident when his car grazed a stag. We talked about the tenuousness of life as we ordered French onion soup and white wine. When the restaurant became too noisy to tape there, we talked about our families. Mariani spoke with affection and pride of his wife, Eileen, and their three sons, Paul, Mark, and John.

After lunch, we continued our conversation in Mariani's office on the campus. As he saw me to my car several hours later, he warned me to be sure to drive very carefully.

Gail Mandell: I know you've just finished a life of the poet John Berryman. What are you working on next? Have you started something else?

Paul Mariani: Nothing at the moment. I have tendinitis in my arm from typing too much. The book is twelve hundred pages, down from seventeen hundred, and I did hurt myself.

What am I working on? Well, I want to get back into poetry. I have half a volume of poems that were held in abeyance while I worked on the Berryman. I'm half finished with that, and I'd like to see if I can get into that mind set again for about a year. As far as another biography, I don't know. I promised myself that it would be a couple of years before I got into another major project. I'll do essays. In the future, maybe a biography of Hopkins. I've just finished my *Inferno* with Berryman, and I did my *Purgatorio* with Williams. I did one book early on, on Hopkins, way back in 1970, which is a kind of reading, but I think I'd like to come back to that religious experience "in extremis": How does one maintain a sense of light in a time of darkness? So I might do the Hopkins in a couple of years. But it's open—up for grabs. I'm not going to sign another contract right away like I did as soon as I finished the Williams. I'm going to give myself a little space this time. If I let the poetry go too long, it's going to be gone forever. It's like a gift that doesn't wait. The muse will just knock on somebody else's door.

GM: Clearly, you are a poet. How did you get interested in biography?

PM: Notice the kind of biography I do is of poets. In a sense, I do two things. I do the biography, but I also learn by that kind of intense meditation something about the craft itself. So it pays a double dividend for me. And I usually pick people that I can learn from, either to do something or not to do something in my own work.

GM: Did you do anything special to get ready to write biography, or did you just plunge in?

PM: In fact, I was afraid to do biography. I was actually afraid to do it. I said, "Who the hell am I to do a biography?" I felt that maybe God came down and appointed you to do it. What really happened was, I had been working for years on a kind of biography of a poem—that's really what I was doing—I was going to do just a genesis and creation of Williams' *Paterson.* I turned in a chapter of this to James Raimes, who was then at Oxford University Press—this was about ten, eleven years ago. He called me about a week later and said, "I've read this; it's very good, I like it a lot, but I'm not interested in your doing a biography of a poem. But if you're willing to undertake the man's entire life, if you're willing to do a biography in other words, I'll give you a contract. I'll give you a couple days to think about it." So a couple days later, I said, "Yes, I'll do it." In other words, I was pushed to do it. I'd wanted to do it. I thought it needed to be done, even though I knew there was someone already doing one, so I said, "Yes, I'll do it." I had spent years doing research on Williams. I knew a lot about him. So that was the final incentive. As I look back at it, the Hopkins book, which is a commentary that came out in 1970, was already a plunge in that direction. It was a New Critical reading, but it was impure New Criticism because it had so much of Hopkins' life. I've always been interested in the relationship between the work and the life, but then this just pushed it over the edge. This was the point at which I said either, "No, I won't do that," or "I will do it," and I said, "Yes, I will do it." I spent the next five years—actually four—writing it, and then a year revising it, shaping it, and getting it ready to publish. That's how it happened. So it was easy. Then you're a biographer.

GM: After you've done it.

PM: Yeah, after you've done it, you're a biographer. Then people ask you what you're doing next.

GM: I was prepared for you to say poetry.

PM: You were? Then you got the answer. I really need that meditation. I might even go on retreat again, out to Gloucester or someplace and try to get into that set of mind—you know, it's a particular set of mind. I didn't realize—you see, with the Williams I could do both. At one time, I thought I could do both biography and the poetry, and Williams allowed me to do that. Insofar as you can talk to the dead, he said, "OK, Mariani, go do something else for awhile." But Berryman didn't. Berryman said, "You belong to me. You belong to me." As it got darker and darker, there was nothing else I could do except Berryman.

Nothing else. Nothing. He just took all my energy. So then I said, "Well, in that case, I'm not just a biographer. There's another part of me that has to be answered, that has to be attended to." That's why the only way I can do it is to take a couple years off, and then go back to it.

See, I want to tell you something else. I don't know that I'll, at the end of my life—say I've got another twenty— I don't know that I just want to be known as a biographer. You know what I mean? I want to have a wider designation. I want to be known for the poetry, too. I don't want to be known as a biographer who happened to write poetry, or a critic who happened to dabble in poetry. That's not—it's too serious for me. I mean, I want it all to be good, all of it. People have a tendency to pigeonhole you. They say, "What are you, a biographer? Or are you a critic? Or are you a poet?" Once in a while it would be nice for them to call you a poet-critic, as they did with Randall Jarrell, for example. But for me—I suppose—I love the biography, I dearly love it; but I suppose if they had to do that stupid thing of sectioning you off, then I suppose poetry would be at the top.

GM: Do you find much creativity in writing biography? For you, is that the attraction?

PM: Mmm. I enjoy it. I enjoy not only the writing of it but I enjoy the rewriting of it. Each biography is rewritten four-five-six-seven-eight times. Each time I rewrite it, I understand things I hadn't—I mean, I had the information, but now I see the patterns, the questions, the new questions: "What about this, what about that?" But it's only in the actual process of rewriting it that you can see the patterns. Only then. I don't even know what the pattern is before that, really.

GM: What do you mean by the pattern?

19

PM: By the pattern, I mean what really held his life together. All I've got are these disparate, individual, discrete facts, and a lot of them don't gel at first, or don't completely gel, but as long as I keep working with them, keep looking at them, keep turning them over, then I begin to see a pattern, that is, something at the center of the individual. My sense is that we are fragmented, but I still believe that at the heart of us is something that is a kind of core that is driving at something. It may get waylaid; it may get pushed to one side or the other; it may get frustrated; but there's an essential core, a kind of drama in us, that we try to fulfill. I know it's there, but I can't in the beginning articulate it. It's only later, later, as I go back over it that I begin to see how it all fits.

GM: And would that pattern for Williams be—am I reading the biography right?—his sense of failure, of never being recognized as, or for what, he hoped to be?

PM: That's right: the sense of a guy coming from under. I was fascinated by that, how Williams was a Johnny-come-lately, really. It took him a long time to be recognized, and a great deal of energy went into his perseverance, into continuing to push, into believing in his own work. That was certainly there. Then of course the fascination of the kind of work that he was doing. If he wasn't being heard, he also understood that an awful lot of people in this country weren't being heard: minorities, women. These are catch phrases, but this is in fact what was happening, and so he identified with his patients. He identified with those people. Who was going to speak for them? Certainly, the intellectuals, the privileged, in a sense, were being listened to. They had Pound to talk for them, they had Henry James, they had T. S. Eliot, in a sense. But Williams spoke for me, for my people. That was important.

GM: Was there someone who started you thinking along biographical lines, like a mother or grandmother who was a storyteller?

PM: Most of the family history is gone. I can think of two vacuums, two absences: my grandfathers, neither of whom I ever knew. I know in other cases, the opposite is true, that there are those who have been gifted with their history or traditions. For me, it was mostly an absence. In the absence of literature, that is, the absence of letters, the absence of anything more than a handful of photographs, writing has been an attempt to fill that vacuum.

It's no accident, I think, the people I chose. I chose Hopkins in my dissertation and first book because I was looking for some sort of religious answer from someone whom I truly respected and from someone—a man like myself—who had gone through a time of extremes, and had somehow survived; who had crystallized it in writing of some sort, even though he had undergone a dark night of the soul. I don't know that I would have articulated it like that at the age of twenty-one when I discovered him, but I was immediately enamored of Hopkins. The first time I picked him up, as a senior in college, I had traded with a friend of mine. Each of us was assigned a poet. I was given Yeats. A friend of mine was an Irishman, a supporter of the IRA. He said, "What do I have to do with this English priest?" So I gave him Yeats, and I took the Hopkins. That made all the difference. He was the first figure that I wanted to know more about. So I read everything else about him. It made me want to go on to graduate school. Hopkins was important. Williams was important. He also ministered—to the sick, and he ministered to the poor. To the patient who couldn't pay, he simply said, "No charge." He had his weaknesses, but he also had great strengths.

GM: You mentioned once that you had used Richard Ellmann's biography of James Joyce as a model for yours of Williams. Why?

PM: When I was in graduate school, I read Ellmann. I was very interested in Joyce, and I read Ellmann. I liked his "objectivity," I liked the panoramic range, I liked the epic thrust of it, and I said, "You know, if I'm going to do this thing for Williams, I've got to do the same kind of thing for him." In other words, I think that he's a major figure. I don't think that many people would have a problem with that now, but they did twenty years ago. They really did. When I was in college, nobody taught me Williams. I had one fifty-minute class on a couple of short poems of Williams'. That was as a senior in college. And then nothing in graduate school. Nothing. I discovered Williams because here, at the University of Massachusetts, they told me I had to teach a course in modern poetry. That, and one time when I was in graduate school literally picking up a volume of *Paterson* in a book store and saying—because my mother's family is from Paterson—and saying, "Paterson—who would write about Paterson?" I didn't understand the poem at the time, but I was fascinated that some poet had touched the American dream. I felt it deserved an epic response, and my model for the epic response, for serious biography, was Ellmann's biography of Joyce. Now, I didn't reread Ellmann, sort of like you've seen a good movie and you don't want to see it later on, because you're afraid you'll pick up the flaws. I wanted to go with the energy that I still had from the Ellmann when I read it back in '62 or '64. So I used it without rereading it in terms of size, in terms of notes, et cetera. It was a good book. But I was doing for an American what Ellmann had done for an Irishman. That was really the kind of thing I had in mind.

GM: So it was your attempt to canonize him?

22

PM: Oh, yes. To canonize him. Sure. In fact, I wrote an article in 1970 called "Towards the Canonization of William Carlos Williams." That was the title of it. And that's what I was doing. I know the whole issue of canon is under fire today.

GM: It sure is. Women have something to do with that.

PM: My whole response, if I were in that position, I think would be to add to the canon. What I don't understand is demolishing the canon altogether. OK, let's revise canon, but we need some kind, that is the mind seems to need some kind, of fiction, some kind of order, so let's add to the canon, let's play with it, let's see if this voice can mesh, has something of value to say that's co-equitable, if you will, or coequal—whatever you want to use—with the voices in the canon. Let's not ghettoize. Let's see if it really does stand. Some of them do.

GM: That depends on whether the works can share criteria.

PM: Yes. Then of course the whole question is, what do you do? Like take Tillie Olsen. One of her themes is, "Look, I was a woman who had to raise a family; therefore, I didn't have the time that you might have." But there were an awful lot of men, too, who perhaps would have liked to have been writers but had to—I remember a guy like that who ran a drugstore during and after the depression who fell into the same thing: economic restraint. My father took me out of high school for a while so that I could work in his gas station. So I'm too close to it to look at it completely—I mean, I almost lost it myself. So you try harder. I look at my own family, and I'm the only one—a number of them now have finally got their college degrees, but it was a long struggle and they didn't finish until they were in their thirties. I didn't come from a privileged background. My father was a mechanic; I was the oldest of seven kids. It was harder for me, you understand. But what I said was, "I want the best rules of the game, and then I'll play according to the rules of the game." The game may be changing, but it's too long and involved to try to deal with here.

You know, I picked up Virginia Woolf's *To the Lighthouse* the other day for the first time. I've read her other works, but I'd never read *To the Lighthouse*. People had told me for years to read it. I'd tried to read it when I was a graduate student, but I couldn't get through it. Now that I'm a parent, it was time for me to read it. I couldn't put it down. It's an extraordinary work, one that I think will continue to move me. She belongs right there with everybody else, no special criteria or anything; she just belongs there.

But yeah, there are going to be others who are trying to do for X, Y, or Z what I tried to do for Williams. It seems to me that what they have to do is demonstrate that X, Y, or Z belong in the canon. They have to do the hard work, and they have to demonstrate it. It takes time, because there are just too many voices clamoring.

Take H. D. I studied that generation, and H. D. is a master. So I say, "Who is doing first-rate work on H. D.?" And I've heard virtually everything. The trouble, to me, is that I haven't found a voice that has been able to do for H. D. yet what Hugh Kenner, say, has been able to do for T. S. Eliot or, in another sense, what I've been able to do for Williams. It'll come, but it hasn't come yet. It's like a marriage. It's not only the person, the author himself or herself. I mean, even Shakespeare—if they hadn't had those prompt books, if they hadn't had someone to put those plays together, they might have disappeared. We don't have Shakespeare's manuscripts. There have to be other people who also see the value of the work, and are willing to put their life's blood into it. Anyway, I believe that what happened with Williams

24

will have to happen for black literature, and it is happening for women's literature, and I see it beginning to happen for others coming up—the children of immigrants, for example. I see a whole new school of immigrant literature. They'll also have to be accommodated. And they will. But they're going to also have to do good work. No special pleading. Then you're also going to have to have other people who are willing to put their own time, their own lives on the line, saying, "Look, this is worth reading, and this is why it's worth reading." It takes time. We only have sixty, seventy years to live, and we can't read it all. How many times has something like this happened to you? Somebody shakes you by the lapel and says, "You gotta read this book." You say, "Yeah, yeah, yeah, yeah," but you can't read everything. It sometimes takes two years, three years, five years, right? But then you do.

GM: Is that then the literary biographer's task: to shake people by the lapels? And by doing so, to revise the canon?

PM: Yes and no. We have to make the life worth reading, both in terms of the new information we bring to bear and in the value of the life we present. All lives overlap, finally, don't they? We all eat, sleep, work, love, desire, fear, learn, fail, succeed, grow older, die. Beyond that is the uniqueness of each life—where and when it was lived: in Kyoto, Calcutta, Montreal, Rome, Boston, New York, Laramie, the Okefenokee. I want people to *want* to read about this life because it's interesting, even absorbing.

But I'm also a revolutionary at heart, and I want to get a hearing for this particular writer who's been important to me but perhaps ignored or dismissed by too many. I want Williams up there (he is now, anyway, isn't he?) and I'll see Berryman there, too. And if I had the courage, I'd do Zora Neale Hurston in memory of my grandmother, since the one reminds me of the other.

25

GM: In spite of your classical, scholarly model, I do see you experimenting to some extent with biographical form in the biography of Williams. For example, you begin the biography at the place where Williams' autobiography ended. I thought that was a brilliant idea. It gave a radical twist to the whole thing.

PM: Thank you. I rewrote the opening six times. I had six different scenarios. That didn't just come to me. Then, that one. I said, "Ah, that's it." Because what I was saying in the form was, "That's where he's ending his, but he's left too many things unsaid. So let's start from there. Let's open it up again."

GM: But you do keep some things closed. For example, why are you so vague in the biography about Williams' various lovers and love affairs?

PM: The truth is, I think that the biographer is a kind of confessor and psychiatrist, as well. I know biographers—and I dislike this trait—who want to find out the "dirt." They want to get the dirt in there. Well, everybody has dirt. Everybody. I didn't whitewash the man's life. It's clear that the guy was a womanizer, for example. But I didn't think it was necessary to name all the women—who are still alive, and who have married or remarried, or are part of the family—and to hurt them. I just didn't think I could live with that. It was a moral decision on my part. If there was a need to name a name, I would name it. And I've got notes. Fifty years from now, if they want to know a name, I've got it. It won't be lost. It's there. But I didn't think it would be proper, in 1981, especially after all the help I'd been given especially by the Doc—Doc Williams, Jr. I don't mean that he looked over my shoulder. He didn't. There was no "it's gotta be cleaned up." There was none of that. From a human perspective, I said, "What's it going to matter in most of these cases, what the names are?" Now, that was the way I thought. However, there was one instance that I didn't know about at the time, but I've corrected that since—in a long review that I did for the *William Carlos Williams Review,* which came out last year, a review of a book by a fellow named D. A. Callard. The book is *Pretty Good for a Woman: The Enigmas of Evelyn Scott.* Have you ever heard of Evelyn Scott?

GM: No.

PM: That was exactly my response: "I've never heard of her." It turns out that she was a great novelist in the twenties, by that I mean a very powerful novelist, and wrote a book on the Civil War ten years before *Gone With the Wind.* It's called *The Wave,* and it's better than *Gone With the Wind.* But by 1929, like a lot of other people, particularly women, she simply disappeared. It's only by luck, by serendipity, that this fellow Callard found some of her manuscripts and began to put them together. Now there's a woman in Louisiana who is writing a biography of her. My point is, I had seen this wonderful letter by Scott in which she describes Williams. I thought, "Boy, this woman is right on target." But there was no evidence of who this Scott was; I just didn't know. Later, I discovered a series of letters from Williams to her at Texas. I went through those letters; she had saved them. I did correct that omission. I did write this essay-review, and I explained. In a sense, I think that the biography is ongoing. It's written, but I know that there are several errors. I did the best I could with what I had, but new knowledge keeps occurring.

GM: So you may need to revise the biography of Williams, as Ellmann did of Joyce's?

PM: That's what I'm hoping to do. Exactly. I would like to do that in another ten or fifteen years. One of the things is, as I say, this update of Williams' response to this serious affair with Scott that he had in 1919–1920. I did deal with that issue, but in another place outside of the biography. You could insert the material of the essay into the biography and get further light on Williams in his mid-thirties.

GM: You had the same dilemma, I imagine, with Berryman.

PM: Yes; there, the same thing. In some instances, honestly, when he meets some woman in the library stacks and they copulate right there, it doesn't matter who the woman is, in one sense. It probably didn't even matter to him. Or then, maybe it does. I have this image that these guys are going to meet all of these women when they're dead, and then they're going to have a lot of answering to do. In a sense, they've become wives to them. That would be hell.

GM: Did you decide to use the same form, the same structure you used for Williams, for the Berryman biography?

PM: No, but how would I describe the form? It is chronological, though if I had to shape it, I'd say it's an inverted pyramid. That is, I try to get through the early years where there's so much unreliable information that I'm leery to use it, and then as he gets older, what happens is his memory kicks in and he begins to rethink the earlier episodes. See, I wanted the first chapter to end with the death of his father, and I did end it there. Since he was so interested in Shakespeare, I keep bringing in allusions to *Hamlet*. In a sense, *Hamlet* already structures the book in large part. I do that for deep reasons. I do that as well for things like the betrayal—that is, the betrayal of the mother— the killing of the father. I even half suspect, and I know that Berryman did, that the death of Berryman's father was not a suicide but may have been a murder. And if not exactly a murder, certainly leaving—that is, a rejection by the mother for this other man—was a kind of murder in itself. What happens to Berryman at first is he has a kind of blackout; he can't remember. He doesn't want to remember. It's like a scarring over. Then there are five wasted years. Only later does he begin to slowly go back and try to figure out what happened. Part of the drama of the book is to watch his mind as it tries to understand what happened. So I don't give it away—I don't say, "Here's exactly what happened." I leave it ambiguous, like a detective novel. We are given only the information that Berryman himself has. We must try to see it through his eyes, through the rest of his life, in his literature.

My point is that his major preoccupation in the poetry is to move more and more freely away from a complex symbolist, New Critical reading of poetry and the writing of it in those terms—the way that Blackmur would have understood a text, say, or Eliot, in terms of the impersonality of the creator—and to move more and more towards a naked autobiography. In other words, as he goes through more and more analysis and begins to get in touch with himself, we see him unfolding. The poetry becomes a character, too, in the book. We see the poetry as an attempt at self-exploration, so that it's a very personal kind of thing, and I read the poems as autobiography. I know that there are pitfalls to this method. I know that it's a fiction, and that Berryman's aware that it's a fiction that he's creating; nevertheless, I find that the "development" of the poetry up through 1947 allows for a kind of gradual discovery, till he comes to a certain point where he confronts his mother.

He then becomes an alcoholic, because he wanted to hide it again. Once it becomes clearer to him—the betrayal, the central betrayal—he tries to cover it again. This explains his relationship to women. He never had a satisfactory relationship with any woman. I think it's because he was damaged because of the relationship between his mother and himself. I think that every subsequent relationship was damaged. The spring was busted right from the beginning. Finally, this turned on him. He kept marrying younger women, thinking, "Well, I can shape them and mold them." Rather than confront an equal, he backs up and marries graduate students: that syndrome. You marry a daughter in a sense, finally—to get as far away from the mother as you can. But the daughter grows into the mother, unless you shape her differently.

Finally he did dry out, after twenty-five years or so of alcohol. Then there was just a vacuum. For a while, he thought that God could fill it. Really, what he was doing was even shaping that. He was using God as an artifact, though I don't know that he was aware of it. In other words, he was using God as an aesthetic. Then that fell away. I think that what had happened was that he had truly had a conversion, back into faith, something that I think is prepared for in going over his life. Some people find that the conversion jumps the track. I don't think it does. I think that if you study the life carefully, you find all sorts of evidence that he's leading towards this, towards a return to the father, the father that he'd lost. But then you have the long afternoon of that relationship, in which you've got to learn to be an adult in that relationship, after the first fervor of the conversion. I think at that point, things began to fall apart: the body was falling apart and the third—and final—marriage was falling apart, and he entered into a darkness and he no longer had inner resources to cope. So you simply find everything falling away, even the things he thought he could hold on to indefinitely. For example: "Certainly, even if things are going bad at home and even if my relationship with God is not all it ought to be, at least I've got my teaching. At least, I can get in there and wow them." But what happens if that goes too and you have nothing to back you up? And that's what you see happening to Berryman. Everything collapses.

GM: All his self-definitions, you mean?

PM: Yes, all the ways he defined himself. You see, I think there are two ways to define yourself. I think there are the articulations, and then there are the secret definitions, which you don't talk about but simply expect people to see. "You can see that I'm a good teacher. You can see that I'm an artist." I think that Harold Bloom is right: There are certain things that are so close to the bone that you don't talk about them. They become magic talismans. You don't want to name them, because to name them is to give power to somebody else. When they're gone, then the spring is really busted. Especially if you're prone to suicide, especially if your father has committed suicide, or perhaps been murdered—

GM: That seems to be your inheritance?

PM: That's right. He really broke down when he heard about Hemingway, for example. He broke down publicly. In fact, when they said, "Hemingway died," he said, "The bastard shot himself, didn't he?" He knew immediately, because he himself had obviously been thinking about it.

GM: Some biographers have talked about the problems of trying to integrate criticism and critical writing with the narrative art of storytelling in biography. Have you found that a problem? Are the two types of writing inimical to each other?

PM: No. I differ from that point of view. My whole sense is to find the fascinating ways in which Berryman, for example, retells in many forms the same stories, but not just to reduce it to *the* story. The story may be the germ, but what I'm also interested in is what else he is doing with it. What sort of structures and forms are in a sense used to distance himself from it. It gives him a way to deal with it, and to create some new reality. And perhaps to discover for the first time, what is the significance of the thing—the tale—which has already happened.

GM: But might it have worked for you because your subjects' work was pretty much autobiographical? Would such integration work in the lives of most writers?

PM: Good question, and the answer to that is: You have to look at each individual life and see what's going to work. I can't do a general diagnosis. I have to do an individual diagnosis. My sense is that in every case, you can have a unique diagnosis and therefore a different way of dealing with the work. You see, I believe in organic form with a biography rather than a set form. Someone asks, "How do you write a biography?" Well, that's a very difficult question to answer. I mean, you have a beginning, a middle, and an end. But maybe there's another way of doing it. Maybe you begin with a false ending. There are all kinds of aesthetic structures that one can use. With Williams there was one. With Berryman, I begin, "Oklahoma." First word: "Oklahoma," because what we forget is the guy came from a "half-savage" country, in Pound's sense. We keep thinking of him as an Eastern aesthete, but there was this whole other element that has to be addressed in some way. So I decided to tell it quick, whack it, I mean to tell the first twelve years in a flash, which is how he remembered it. These are aesthetic issues that can only be dealt with as you actually work with the material. You've got to be right down there wrestling with it.

GM: You work with so many sources of information when you're writing a biography. Which was the most valuable for you?

PM: The papers—the papers from the times. I really don't trust memory. What happens with Williams and Berryman are two things, at least. Some people, now that he's a famous man, don't want to upset the applecart. They just want to say nice things about him, and so they falsify the record. Or they're still angry about something. It may be a stupid little thing, like in the case of Williams, not giving a nephew ten dollars when he thought he deserved ten dollars. Williams didn't even know the nephew expected the money. But the guy's never forgotten it, even though now he's a millionaire. It can be weird, what happens.

And then people just forget. I notice that in my own life. I did a poem. My mother's got lung cancer. My brother Walter and I went up to see her. In this new book of poems—you mind if I talk about the poems for a minute? You see, in the house where we grew up in Mineola, my brother, who's a frustrated artist, did a charcoal of a Winslow Homer painting for a class. All these years, in my memory was one seascape, a seascape of a single sailor, a fisherman on the Maine coast, with two large flounder with a typhoon coming. You've probably seen this; it's a famous one. That's the one I thought he did. I'm in the apartment, talking with my mother, and Walter's with me, and on the wall she's got the picture. She's taken it as one of the few possessions she still has. And it's not the picture. In other words, the picture my brother did was of two men in a boat. It was by Winslow Homer, but a different scene altogether, and you can't see the flounder in the boat. In my mind, I had substituted, and I was convinced—absolutely convinced by what I remembered. If that can happen to me and I'm a "biographer"! Why did that happen? Why did I substitute? And not only that, but create a poem, so that I then re-created it?

People are doing this all the time with Berryman and Williams. For example, one of Berryman's former students told me that when he was teaching at Rochester, they had brought Berryman in for a reading, and he was really in bad shape. Now another of Berryman's former students happened to be in Rochester at the same time, and he insisted that Berryman was in good shape and was quite articulate and that they had this discussion, but the first guy said that Berryman could hardly talk. So what do you do? Here is the same incident, and you have two conflicting pieces of information. And you're continually running into that. In that case, what I did was take a third source, plus I looked at what had happened as soon before that as I could and as soon after. And I realized that the first guy's memory in this particular case seemed to be more solid. You see what happens? I have to make a choice. Now I wasn't there, so I'm well aware that what I'm creating is a fiction. I mean, I think it's true, it seems to fit, but maybe he sobered up. But I doubt it. The guy was too far gone. I mean, he was drinking too much. He was packing bourbon in his suitcase, like W. H. Auden at the end, and if you're drunk, you're drunk for a while. It made sense to follow this, but I had no absolute evidence of any of it. You try, with all the disparate pieces, to make the most palatable life you can, but realizing always that you're telling a story, and because it's a story, it's a fiction. There's no way out of that. It's always got to be interpretation.

GM: But you did a lot of interviewing, I presume. What did the interviews give you?

PM: What were some of the things that were most important to me? The interviews with the wives were too emotion-packed. Eileen Simpson was trying too hard, even in *Poets in Their Youth,* which is a study of Berryman and Lowell. I think that she's not telling the whole truth there, and it bothers me because she's a trained psychologist. I just don't think she told the truth—it's an avoidance tactic. She just couldn't tell what really happened. It was much grubbier than she let on. The study is sort of like looking at a James Bond movie. James Bond has just had a fight for his life with this guy and doesn't even have to straighten his tie. In a real fight, there's a lot more blood drawn than that. With Eileen, you never get the sense that a hair is messed. The worse thing is that when she found out that someone was doing the biography, she called Kate, the third wife, and demanded Berryman's diaries and journals for the years 1942–56. They don't belong to her! She and Berryman were divorced in 1956. But Kate had them turned over. So there's this terrible hiatus.

GM: What did you do about those gaps?

PM: I had to fill in with other things. I had to go to every other source I possibly could and fill in. But I would love to have those diaries, if they still exist. She says they do. So anyway, when I wrote to her to thank her for the interview, I said, "Look, you know that I've got to ask you for the diaries. You know I've got to see at least a section of the diaries; I've got to have a section to corroborate, right?" And I even said, "I'll show you the stuff that I'm writing. I can't give you the last word on it," I said, "but I'm not out to hurt you in any way. I've got to tell the story." No answer. Period. No answer. You win some, you lose some. That was my big loss. That was the only outstanding, only major one. I have another small loss. The second wife of Robert Fitzgerald wants to hold on to the letters until she can get money for them. She feels badly but . . . I said, "OK, look, don't feel badly. I can't wait forever." That kind of thing happens sometimes. But I have so much material. As I say, the biography was seventeen hundred pages, and I knocked that down to twelve hundred and fifty. It's in the editor's hands now. Maybe it'll be cut. I can't see it being cut much more than that, though. I'll have to see how that works. If it doesn't work, I'll just have to get another editor. That's written in my contract.

GM: About the papers themselves: why are they your favorite source?

PM: Because you've got the stuff written in the heat of the moment. You have it written right then. And though something might be written with the writer having in the back of his mind posterity, he won't always be doing that. There will be crises, and he'll write what's on his mind. You've got it right there; you've got the artifact from 1946. You've got it in the language of 1946. You don't have it in the language of 1987, which already is altered and changed. You see, the language itself is a character, and one of the ways you can really get the life is to bring in the language of the moment. If you're writing the biography of a woman in the nineteenth century, say, a New England woman, from Lowell, Massachusetts, working in the mills, part of what's going to matter is the specific language, even the misspellings, and her perceptions at that moment. Even the words that have dropped out of the vocabulary. I think we have to at least address the language, which is itself setting up land mines and revelations.

I'm very much one for the historical texture. I want the 1936 Buick that Berryman is driving. When Berryman is racing to see his brother, who's been in an accident, I want to get the tick of that car, of the '36 car as it races across the Wisconsin landscape then. I want to get a sense of that moon, over those woods, at that moment. If the fan belt's off, if I can find that, if the fan belt's making a tick, I want to know that. I want to get those sensory perceptions into the book. Not just the mind, 'cause we don't live with just minds. We live with tendinitis, we live with limps, we live with periods, we live with headaches, and that's going to affect the very way that we're proceeding—the great abstractions.

36

GM: Did you change anything about the way you collected material or put it together from the time you did the Williams to the time you did the Berryman? In other words, did you learn anything from the first biography that you then applied to the second?

PM: Yeah, I did. I learned how to speed up. With Williams, I had made a lot of detours. I found I spent a lot of time and legwork for bad interviews with people who didn't have any real information, finally, to share, or couldn't recover it.

The fact of a computer has helped me. In terms of the revisions, it's probably saved me literally months. Just the technological advances have helped. Everything I did for the Williams was on three-by-five cards, which I then typed onto a sheet and then had to move around, you see. And this was on my wife's little portable, which I burned out, literally. But I was obsessed with the biography, so it didn't matter. I was going to do it, come hell or high water. But the computer has certainly helped me in terms of the revision, in terms of building up the notes, which I can then put onto a copy and then take the notes and begin to write my first draft from the notes and then begin to revise for style.

I think I learned when to go for an interview and when not; that if I could find primary sources in libraries where those were available—and they were—to go and to use those first. I just learned a lot of shortcuts in terms of what seemed to be important to put down, and what not. What that means, though, is there's got to be at least a preconception. I'll tell you something. I remember with the Williams, I thought I had a preconception about Williams, and so I would copy out certain information and let other information go. And then as I learned more about Williams, I found that some of the information that I let go was very important, and that it was twice as hard to recover it then. So what I do now is have a wider sense of what is important, then I can let it go later.

GM: What about working with a publisher? Did it change the books in ways you would have preferred not to have them change? Or did it improve them in any way?

PM: I told you what happened with James Raimes, about the Williams. That was a major change, right there. Then I had an unfortunate experience, because one of my editors was an alcoholic and he had to be, not let go but put on vacation for a while. He was a good man, a sweet man. I wish I could have worked with him, but he simply was not responding to correspondence and things like that, so that simply wasted time. Then I got a young woman, and the problem there was that I was able to bully her, and that's not good. That is, I was older, I was the authority, and she went very, very lightly with the changes. In some ways, I wish in retrospect that she had wrestled harder with me on them. My present editor is still an unknown quantity, and I'm a little afraid, because I've heard—others have not had happy experiences—but I'm giving her the benefit of the doubt. We'll see. At this point I wait, to see what the returned manuscript is going to look like. What she's said so far has made sense. She said, "These early chapters need to be reshaped," and that's true. I think as you write, you get better as you go along, so I'm not surprised that the earlier chapters perhaps need to be cut back—you know, the high-school years. That is, what I thought was so important, from another person's perspective might not be so important. And I need that, I need someone else. Just like with my poems. I'll do my poems until I can't do them any more, then I'll give them to a poet to look at with a fresh eye. I just sent one of my poems to Phil Levine, and Phil sent back wonderful criticism, and I followed his criticism, and it shaped the poem. Just like Eliot took *The Waste Land* and gave it to Pound, and Pound cut that thing in half. You do all the work—it's all there—but you need someone else's eye sometime.

GM: Did you work out a theory of what a life is, some idea of the nature of the self, before you started writing, or did that come after, or has it come at all? Do you just tell the story?

PM: I'm not a theoretician. I don't think I am. I may well be, but somebody else is going to have to articulate it. Clearly there are things working there, and I'm almost afraid to name them myself. I'm skittish of theory; it's almost too restrictive for me. I don't have that kind of mind; I have, if you will, more an artist's intuitive mind. But I work hard. I mean, if I hear that there's a letter here or there, I'll go after it. I do the legwork. I don't try to skimp. I don't try to mythologize. I try to get all the hard evidence that I can. If I can visit the places—all of that. I try to get a sense of all of that. But I guess what I'm trying to do is to discover something in the unfolding of the material. I try to listen hard to what it wants to tell me, you understand, or what Berryman wants to tell me. I don't want to impose on it. There have been enough critical studies of these men—and of everyone, really—and I don't like them, I don't like them. Essentially they're Procrustean beds. When it's time to talk about a theory, I'll bring that theory in, but no one's going to know where that stuff is coming. You turn the page in the Williams, and there may be something on the Spanish Civil War, and how you get medical supplies there, even though three pages earlier it may be something about the attempt to do *Contact* magazine. I want it to unfold the way the life unfolded. Do we know what will happen tomorrow? We think we do. There's an excitement about both man's puny plans for himself or herself, and then the reality, which is refreshing, exciting, better than whatever we planned.

GM: So you wouldn't call yourself a Freudian, say?

39

PM: No, not exactly, but I do find myself in a kind of ersatz way going back to Freud. His model seems to make sense to me. But I don't like to use the terminology. You'll see the darkness of these people I write about, that they're doing what appear to be irrational things, but I don't think they're actually irrational. I think Freud's right, I don't think that anything is finally an accident. I think that there are reasons why people are doing certain things. I think the thing is to uncover them. So I am being like a psychoanalyst, an amateur psychoanalyst. I listen carefully, and the patterns do begin to grow. You asked me before about the pattern. It's clear after a while that Berryman hates himself; he's a very unhappy man. He marries his first wife, who loved this man. Why didn't it work out? She was willing to sacrifice. She took menial jobs, et cetera; she loved the guy. But he didn't love himself, and it wasn't enough. Why? Why didn't he love himself? Was there something else? You had to go back. Was he shown love by his mother? Then you find that at one point, he said, "Although she showed me a lot of attention, she never showed me love." It's that primal scene. With Berryman, it has to be Freud, because Berryman himself was undergoing Freudian analysis. That made sense to me.

With Williams—Williams never studied Freud. I mean, he read Freud and Jung, but he read them in the little magazines as literature. What you find with him is a man not in touch with himself—oh, in some ways, yes, but in other ways wildly wrong.

GM: Then you wouldn't accept the person's interpretation of himself or events in preference to a judgment you yourself would make on his or her life?

PM: No. I can't do that. Why? Let's take the question of fidelity. Williams continually, right to the end of his life, was sorry for what he had done when he realized he had

40

hurt his wife. But that's not enough for him. He also has to try to explain, to make an apology, a defense, for his actions. Floss didn't buy it, and the truth is, I don't buy it. So what I do, I don't come in heavy-handedly and say, "Williams was a jerk"; what I do is simply show you his wife's ashes being scattered. That speaks eloquently, I think. You explain that one. That was her response. So I will set up those sorts of patterns.

Clearly, for Berryman to jump, there has to be some kind of an explanation. I remember literally trembling at the typewriter as I wrote. I had to stop, I had to go to sleep, then wake up and do it by pages, a page, a page and a half, because literally the goose bumps were raised. I was about to lose the man, and I kept saying, "John, don't do it." It's already history. It's like a Greek tragedy. You know what's going to happen. It's like *Hamlet*. At the end of the fifth act, no matter what you want Hamlet to do, he's going to die. The same thing with Berryman.

But no. I try not to impose. But that's not the whole story. There are value judgments; just the way I put sequence after sequence is a value judgment. But I try not to do it overtly. One of the major things in the Berryman biography is his alcoholism. Now, I've worked with alcoholics. My own mother was an alcoholic until about ten years ago. That makes her still an alcoholic, but she's in recovery. And my grandmother died an alcoholic, so it's something that has been close to me. You watch it, and you know how people in that situation lie to themselves. In a way, I will simply allow the narrative to make the point. I have Berryman saying how he's not going to drink heavily any more, he's only going to have four martinis. The fact that I put that in there would, I would assume, cause anybody to conclude the obvious. I don't have to say, "Obviously, Mr. Berryman was fooling himself by taking those four martinis." It's indirect, but it's there.

GM: I know that you are a practicing Catholic. Do your religious values come into play as you write these lives, or interpret them?

PM: I try not to let them. But a good friend of mine who's a poet once said to me, "You know, Mariani, I think I know why you're interested in biography." He's a very devout Anglican. He said, "I think it's because of the importance of the Incarnation in your life. That is, the reality of the Incarnation, which therefore informs the drama of every individual's life. A life is not meaningless, and it's more than just a story: its authenticity comes from its spiritual dimension, even if the person's not aware of this. You are trying to find the drama, that search for a deeper sense of oneself in the life." I thought about that, and it made a lot of sense.

I do think we either look for happiness or we condemn ourselves. I know there are some happy people out there and an awful lot of unhappy and confused people out there. I suppose you could use a metaphor and say they're moving towards a kind of light. I know that Williams uses that metaphor, and Berryman speaks of light and darkness. I don't suppose you can avoid altogether some of that religious tenor. Berryman is clearly moving towards trying to regain his Catholic faith. He was raised a Catholic and lost it for many, many years then returns to it. Williams was a different case. His mother was a Catholic, but she scared him because he also saw her doing séances and that kind of irrational thing. Williams was always afraid of the irrational. He didn't want to get into any of that. He wanted to try to make it all make sense in terms of a scientific model. But the reason you do that, I think, is that you have an underlying fear of the things that you can't explain. So those kinds of judgments certainly come in.

Certainly, I'm trying not to do hagiography, although Harold Bloom did say I did kind of an idealized version of Williams. That may be true, there may be a little bit of truth in that, because I loved the man. There are biographers who seem to hate their subjects, and they're out to really defile them. They want to defile the people; they want to spit on the corpse. I can't understand it. I'm not kidding. I don't want to name any names, but some people—I'd like to throttle them, because the subject can't respond. My own sense is, if there's a choice between thinking good of a person and thinking evil, I'll always go for the good, just put the best possible interpretation on things, because we'll all be judged—by God or our readers.

Conversation with

Arnold Rampersad

Arnold Rampersad lives in an apartment on Manhattan's West Side, close to the Hudson River. He invited me to meet him there late one afternoon, explaining that he was on leave from teaching that semester and worked all day at home. He was at the time finishing up the second volume of his two-volume *Life of Langston Hughes*. Reading the first volume had sent me in search of its author.

Rampersad and I sat in his airy living room, which, thanks in part to the bright works of art on the white walls, conveyed something of the spirit of his native Trinidad. His American wife made tea for us, which we sipped as we talked. She and a daughter occasionally passed through the room on their way to other parts of the apartment. At one point, Rampersad excused himself to check on a crying baby; he came back with his infant son, Luke, whom he stood holding until the baby quieted down.

After our conversation, his wife (the rest of the family having already eaten by then) served us a splendid meal. Sitting at either end of the dining room table, we talked about teaching biography and autobiography, which he has done most recently at Stanford and Rutgers, and now does at Columbia.

Gail Mandell: At the very end of your biography of Langston Hughes, you say that shortly after being introduced to the executor of Hughes' estate, you were asked to write the authorized biography. Why do you think you were chosen?

Arnold Rampersad: I'm sure there were many reasons. The reason given at the time was that I had done a biography of W. E. B. Du Bois. Actually, I don't think that book and the Hughes book are very similar. I called the Du Bois book, which was titled *The Art and Imagination of W. E. B. Du Bois,* an "intellectual biography." I've since joked that an intellectual biography is what you write when you don't have access to the papers. I now think an intellectual biography is very much a poor cousin of full biography. But that was the reason given by the executor, that he had read that book and thought I'd done a good job on Du Bois's life, linking the life and the art, and so he thought I would probably do something good with Langston Hughes. Obviously, if that was the model in his mind for the ideal Hughes biography, I didn't live up to it. I think I did something quite different from the Du Bois book. But that was why I was asked—as far as I know. He may have had some other factors under consideration, but that's the only one I know about.

GM: Before I met you, I wasn't aware that you were a native of Trinidad. Did you find it difficult to enter into the experience of someone from another culture?

AR: No, I don't think so. A person's particular background is only one aspect of a biography. I've never felt that coming from another part of the world in any way invalidated my status as a biographer. Of course, I had been in this country by that point some fifteen years. I was a student of American literature and of Afro-American literature, and all of that made me familiar with Langston Hughes.

In fact, in writing the biography of a poet such as Langston Hughes, it would be of greater assistance if you had been close to a major poet—any good poet—and I was fortunate at one time to be close to someone who was a poet and dramatist of some stature. It's likely that makes up for other deficiencies.

GM: How much did you know of Langston Hughes before you undertook the project?

AR: Very little. I'd known him enough to admire him, and I knew he had a lot of work out there. That was one of the things I liked about him, the challenge of dealing with an author who had many books.

GM: Had you ever met Langston Hughes?

AR: I never met him. I listened to him on tapes; I saw him occasionally on film. That was about it. What I saw on film and heard on tape did not inspire me particularly. But his writings did, especially his correspondence—the more unguarded aspects of his output. He seemed to me very clearly to be a man of great integrity, and I admired that and felt that I had an obligation to him.

GM: One of the strengths of the book, I think, is the way you create his milieu—for example, the Kansas of his boyhood, the Harlem of his youth. How did you gather the information that would allow you to bring those places and periods to life?

AR: The first thing is research. In the case of Lawrence,

Kansas, I went to the local historical society and discovered as much as I could about life in Lawrence. I read the newspapers of the period to see what life was like in Lawrence at that time. Then there is also luck: finding people who have a really firsthand knowledge of the areas and can assist you. Again in the case of Lawrence, there were two or three people there who had lived in Lawrence for a very long time, some of them all their lives, and who also had a scholarly interest in Lawrence. What you have to do is draw on those people as much as you can.

I also think empathy is very important. It's not enough to be there physically. Even reading the newspapers and so on, you have to dig deep in yourself and try to empathize with the particular community—not resist it—but enter into its mind, insofar as a community has a mind. So you have to work at it. You have to realize that it's extremely important if you're going to understand the individual to understand something of the communities that produced him.

GM: How far did you travel to retrace Hughes' footsteps?

AR: I traveled pretty far. I guess the farthest I went in the case of Langston Hughes was Samarkand in Soviet Central Asia. I went to Tashkent, Samarkand, Leningrad—all in the Soviet Union. I think that was the farthest place.

That's interesting as a proposition—how much you actually get from going to a place where your character has been but for which you have no really original material to connect him to that place. To this moment I'm not sure what I got from standing outside the tomb of Tamerlane in Samarkand, for example; I only know that Hughes talked about being there on his last evening in Soviet Central Asia. I went there, stood outside the tomb, looked about, tried to get past the modernization to what it must have been then. The only thing that I'm certain about is that I'm a better biographer of that particular incident or episode in his life for having been there. You *have* to have a little bit more insight—not much more, but a little bit more—for having been in an exotic place where your character has been rather than not going there at all but simply working out of a printed page or a handwritten letter, for example.

GM: Were you given grants to travel, or was it your own undertaking?

AR: Now and then I had grants, but in any case, I was going to spend my money. I was not going to let money stand in the way of taking any step I needed to research the biography. As long as I had the money. Once I had established a goal or identified a move that I needed to take in order to better understand Hughes, I would take that move, no matter what it cost me.

GM: Did you pursue the same approach with Du Bois?

AR: The Du Bois book was a very limited operation. I wanted principally to understand his books and to draw from them a coherent picture of the mind—also, a just picture of the mind—because I felt that people who had written about Du Bois up to that point had misrepresented him and did not understand how very special his intelligence was—its range—and didn't quite understand why a book such as *The Souls of Black Folk* had the enormous impact on black intellectual life that it did.

GM: How do you account for your change in approach and attitude between the first biography and the second?

AR: There were two different goals. One was a narrow book, the other was a full-scale biography, a broad book. There was also a difference in raw material. In the first instance, I did not have access to the Du Bois papers. Perhaps I would have done something more like the Langston Hughes biography with Du Bois if I had had access to the papers, but they were sealed, pretty much locked up at the time, being edited by someone else. In the case of Langston Hughes, not only were the papers open to me, but they were voluminous, a tremendous archive. Once you have that tremendous archive, it makes certain types of biography possible; whereas if you have a very small archive and you have to hunt for basic letters, you're going to write something that is radically different from the biography you write with a large archive.

Also, I had grown up. I had become older and, I presume, more worldly, and I began to be interested in different questions. Academically, too, I was further along. I mean, I was less concerned with impressing fellow scholars. I could begin to do the business of biography, which I think is narrating a life in as interesting a way as possible.

GM: So you think that biography is basically storytelling?

AR: Certainly I would say that it's storytelling. I think it varies from person to person, but if the subject has led a very interesting and varied life, then I think that the biographer has an obligation to replicate that life in a sparkling—one hopes a sparkling—narrative. If the subject has been dull and has been, say, a scholar, without any particular human verve, then you don't—you can't—make a silk purse out of nothing.

GM: I'm curious about your interest in biography. How did it begin?

AR: As long as I can remember, I've been interested in the combination of history and literature. My definition of biography is simply the history of an individual. People worry about definitions of biography, but I think it's very simple: the history of an individual. It's a branch of *history*. Nothing else, really.

GM: Do you approach a life as you might a historical subject?

AR: I think so. I'm not a trained historian, however, and maybe I'm wrong to approach it that way, but yes, I approach it as I think historical subjects ideally should be approached, and as we understand it now (we didn't understand it thirty years ago), that takes into account every branch of learning, from psychology to aesthetics. I mean, if you want to write a history of a town, for example, you will be doing it correctly only if you become involved in every discipline, every branch of learning.

GM: To your way of thinking, then, biography is interdisciplinary?

AR: It's certainly as interdisciplinary as good history should be. I think it's essentially interdisciplinary, yes. Of course, not every discipline is involved in every biography, but certainly the basic ones of history, sociology, literature, and psychology are definitely involved.

GM: Are there biographies that you particularly like, which have influenced you?

AR: I like the ones that most would call the great biographies, ones that are highly regarded like Leon Edel's *Henry James* and Richard Ellmann's life of James Joyce. Like those biographers, I was committed to a detailed biography and I was also determined as far as I could to carry the reader along with a strong narrative. Every time I felt the book coming to a halt because of something that seemed tremendously significant or portentous, I looked again because I think the essential thing is to keep the reader moving along.

Also, I'm a great admirer of R. W. B. Lewis's *Edith Wharton*. In fact, when I was beginning the Langston Hughes book, that was the biography that had the greatest impact on me. It had come out not so long before. I admired the book, knowing all along that a biography of Langston Hughes could not be too much like a biography of Edith Wharton because they were such different people. I admired the seamlessness of the Lewis book, and its appropriateness of tone—also its complexity of tone. In a sense, reading it was like reading a Jamesian narrative, although it was very clear, much clearer than a lot of Henry James.

I liked the Hemingway biography, as well, the one by Carlos Baker, although I think perhaps—but I wouldn't want to criticize it. I would simply say that his biography reflects my idea—and I'm sure it's a commonly held idea—that a literary biography should in some way reflect the aesthetic qualities of the work of the subject. Not that it should be a kind of mirror image of the writer's art, but in some way it should suggest it. I think the Baker book goes quite a distance in doing that. Specifically, Hemingway's tough-guy pose and prose definitely invade the biographical form as Baker interpreted it. That's very effective, I think.

GM: What of Langston Hughes' work did you study to capture his style in your biography?

AR: That's a good question. In fact, I think my book is quite unlike Hughes' basic style in many ways. On the other hand, I think Hughes would have been quite capable of reading my book and enjoying it from an objective distance. Hughes emphasized simplicity in his art, and I don't think that I ever took simplicity—I mean radical simplicity—as an important criterion for my book. I wanted as many people as possible to read and understand it, but I think the intelligence, such as it is, behind my biography is much more sophisticated and complex than Hughes usually generates or allows to enter his own narratives. That doesn't mean, of course, that it's superior to Hughes' intelligence. You understand that.

Let me make this point, that Hughes' simplicity is often held against him. People don't see the complexity; they don't see the richness of his mind; they don't see how so many of the things he did were done by choice, not simply because he didn't know better or couldn't do something else. So at one and the same time, I had to honor Hughes' intelligence—that deep intelligence he did not always allow into his work—and also cohere with his sense of an audience, his sense of wanting to reach a great number of people. Particularly in the matter of race. And you always have to talk about race when you talk about Langston Hughes. I mean, his sense that he wanted to reach the masses of black people and had to make them see themselves in highly positive ways.

GM: Did you have a specific audience in mind for your biography of Langston Hughes?

AR: I was trying to straddle many audiences. I wanted to write a book that my colleagues in the department would like and admire, but also I wanted to write a book that the typical readers of Langston Hughes would be able to read. And I'm amazed at the number of people who tell me, "I've read your book," or "I've read a good deal of your book." To me it's a big challenge to read all of a long book, and I'm surprised at the many people who seem to have done so. But I did not want to write a book that only scholars would admire. Nor did I want to write a popular book that scholars would not admire. Notation, for example—this is one way you can pinpoint this matter. I didn't care at all about giving notations to background material; I wanted to keep the notes to a minimum. I'm glad that I was able to keep note numbers out of the text. I simply gave the source of actually quoted material. For example, I didn't say, "For the background of Harlem in the 1920s, see Gilbert Osofsky." I wanted to avoid pedantry as much as possible.

GM: Do you think that the audience for whom Hughes was writing could appreciate your biography of him?

AR: He wrote for a fairly wide audience. I'm not sure.

GM: In one passage of the biography, you point out that Hughes wanted to be a black poet, not a poet who happened to be black.

AR: Indeed, in 1926, he stated frankly that unlike some young black poets, who wanted to be considered poets first and blacks afterwards, he felt the two things were one, really, in his case—and in their case.

GM: About yourself as a biographer—do you think of yourself as a black biographer, or as a biographer who happens to be black, who happened to choose a black subject? In other words, did you want to bring a black consciousness to your work?

AR: No, no, I didn't have any sense of myself as a black biographer. I was interested, however, in representing the truth. I was aware, or at least I believed very strongly, that whole aspects of life that I regarded as being intrinsic to the black experience had as far as I'm concerned hardly ever been represented in biographies, in histories. I wanted to show as far as I could, again by using details, by developing character and so on according to standards of accuracy without inventing, to show something of what I considered the greater richness of black life at a certain level: the level, say, of the black poets in the twenties aspiring to become great world poets—maybe failing—but young artists setting out boldly with a vision of themselves and the world that had not been adequately represented. I absolutely wanted to paint a portrait of the black community, or that thin slice of it that involved Langston Hughes, that had never been published before, at least as far as I'm aware.

I don't know that I had any special entrée into it. I think, however, that it did help that I had the sense that this quality had never been represented and that I wanted it shown. Another person without the same sense of obligation or urgency might easily have taken shortcuts. In fact, many another biographer who happened to be black might not have seen this lack as a question or a problem. Many of them might not have taken it on as an issue. But I certainly was sensitive to it and have always been sensitive to it, without considering myself in any way particularly political.

GM: I suppose the same thing could be true of a woman writing the biography of another woman. Even if one isn't political, isn't a committed feminist, she perhaps has an obligation to raise certain issues, address certain lacks.

AR: Yes, especially in the matter of women's interior lives. So many biographies and histories have been written ascribing very little to women's interior lives except in very conventional ways—in particular, ascribing very little to women's intellectual lives. Now all that has changed. The mind of a woman is now certainly on the same level as the mind of a man as a field of investigation for the scholar, the biographer. New terms are being invented and developed—a whole new way of approaching the subject. That's what I was trying to do for black American culture.

GM: You've just finished the second volume of the

Hughes biography, which is not yet published. What's it like to write a life in stages? For example, how did you decide on the length of each volume, and where a good stopping point would be?

AR: In the first place, I decided that I would not try to keep it to any length. I would write the biography in first draft—that was the goal. I would just write. I hand wrote it. The chapters kept ending at wonderful places. The material just seemed to order itself. I guess I should give myself a little bit more credit. But before a chapter could become too long, an ending presented itself—a dramatic ending, because I was determined that the book would be dramatic. Each chapter should end ideally on a note that piques the interest and pushes the reader to move on to the next. So I wrote the entire two volumes. I didn't know it was going to be two volumes; I thought I was writing one volume. Then I thought to myself, "This book is too long. I want to rewrite it entirely one more time. I want to check all the facts and expand the areas that are insufficient in some way." Then I said, "This means it's more than one volume." By that time, two years had passed since I had started out. I spoke to a colleague of mine, a senior scholar, and I asked him whether he thought I should wait and bring out both volumes together. He said, "Absolutely not. Anyone speaking pragmatically and professionally would tell you to turn out a volume at a time." So I said, "All right, I'll turn it out." And I saw immediately where the best place to break the book would come.

I chose to break the book at the point where Hughes was at the absolute lowest in his life. Which was itself a little daring, I guess. But I had seen the end of the story, so I knew that he would come back. I thought that was the best place to end the first part of his story, where the normal reader would be tremendously piqued, have his curiosity raised as to what would happen in volume two.

GM: How was it, with the first volume completed and unable to be changed, to go on with the second?

AR: It was relatively easy, because I had written both volumes in draft. But in fact what was originally volume two in the first draft doubled in size, so the second volume now is quite different from the first draft.

I think it would have been extremely difficult to have begun volume two without some knowledge, more or less, of exactly where I was going. In the course of revising what I had written already, I made major changes, and I saw things differently in some substantial ways. I had originally written those chapters that became the second volume as a falling off of the story. Once I decided to do two volumes, then I had to conceive of it not as a falling off but as a story unto itself, or as a volume unto itself. I didn't want to cheat, but when I looked more closely at the story I saw that, yes, it was a volume unto itself. On the other hand, I don't think it's as interesting a volume. I shouldn't be saying that, but I don't think it's as interesting. Nevertheless, I don't think you have to be uniformly interesting when you do a multi-volume work. You can't really be much more interesting than the life is interesting. If the life is less interesting, then that will be reflected in your biography.

GM: Some artists peak young. Do you think that was true of Langston Hughes?

AR: In many respects, I think that all artists peak young. I think if you examine the record you'll see that not all, but most do.

GM: Surely Keats—though we have no clue what would have happened later.

AR: No, we don't know what would have happened, but

consider Wordsworth, and on and on you go. The great work is done, in fact, in one's youth. But not only that. Biography is not only concerned, or even primarily concerned, with the art but with the life, so far as I'm concerned—not the art but the life. Even though the art may be the reason we write about the person at all. For many of us, in the second half of our lives we're not as interesting. We're more set, we take fewer chances, we're less vulnerable, we work very hard to make ourselves less fragile. We become dull, comparatively speaking. In our youth, we're more interesting. That's certainly been the case with Langston Hughes for me. He took fewer chances; he was less vulnerable in the second half of his life. Yet still I have to tell the story.

GM: You've said that Hughes' autobiographies are the source of a great deal of misinformation about him. How did you satisfy yourself that you were rectifying those distortions?

AR: There are two levels on which they are at times inaccurate. One of them is simply the factual level. The other involves the spirit of the autobiography. An autobiographer is not obliged to be particularly accurate as to facts. It's the business of a biographer to be accurate, but not an autobiographer. An autobiographer has to represent a spirit.

Because of the archive and other research, I was able to look at the autobiographies and see where the facts were plumb wrong, where sometimes Hughes had changed them but sometimes misremembered them. Then there's the question of the spirit. Hughes, who was pretty guarded as a character in revealing his inner self, altered the texture of certain experiences for the autobiographical moment for one reason or another. In the case of his first autobiography, *The Big Sea,* when he was talking about his father and his mother, I was able to read between the lines and point out how he was deliberately sending messages to his readers that he hoped would make them see him in a certain light in relation to his race. But for a lot of his autobiographical writing—in particular, almost the entire second volume—he was not sending any of those messages; he was, however, concealing whole areas of his personality and character because he didn't think they were especially appropriate to the kind of autobiography he wanted to write. Rather than autobiography, he wrote something like memoirs in *I Wonder as I Wander.* However, it seems to me that in the first one, however willy-nilly, he did reveal the way he saw himself as a poet, the way he felt about his father and his mother, the way he felt about his loneliness, about his having been abandoned as a child. He let this out—it came out—mainly, I think, because of the power of the autobiographical form, which is not easily controlled. Just as art is not, just as poetry and prose are not easily controlled by the artist.

GM: Did the autobiographies hinder your research more than they helped?

AR: In the long run, yes, I would say they hindered more than they helped, not only because of the inaccuracy of facts, which was a relatively slight problem, but also because of what I was saying—manipulations of the spirit, so that you would think from reading the autobiography that he saw his life or his experience in a certain way when he didn't. Again and again when writing about the autobiographies as autobiographies, I talk about how they reveal the "blues spirit," which is this business of laughter triumphing over circumstance. Hughes loved the blues, but the laughter could easily make you not see the pain. You don't then see the degree of pain; you don't see the inflictors of the pain. So you don't see that pain is being inflicted on Langston Hughes and you don't see those who inflicted pain upon him. If Hughes is going to joke about Zora Neale Hurston and say, "Oh, girls are funny creatures," or talk briefly about Mrs. Mason—"Godmother"—or hardly mention Alain Locke at all, you can easily be led to believe that they weren't that important, when in fact they were terribly important. Or if he laughs about his mother and seems almost totally unaffected by the way she treated him as a child, then you really go down the wrong path. The burden of my inquiry, especially treating the early years, was to show how he in fact was deeply affected by feelings of isolation and abandonment. That really went straight against the grain of the portrait of himself that he had put forth. A lot of artists show the pain that they have felt in their lives, and milk it, and nurture it, publicly and privately. They show it in terms of paranoia or near-madness. You see them suffering. That was the last thing Hughes wanted you to see: to see him suffering. So a lot of people never saw that he had suffered. That made the biographical task more difficult.

GM: Did the interviews you conducted help much in understanding him?

AR: No, I came away with little or no regard for the interview process. I'm sure I'm too hard on it, but most of my interviews were done after I had gone through the correspondence, which is enormous—over three thousand folders of manuscript material alone. The inaccuracy of fact in the interviews was quite startling. How people would invent for you! Subsequent to talking to people, I would say there are three kinds of interviews: one, with people who know something, and don't want to help you; another with those who know something and want to help you; finally, most dangerous of all, with those who don't know anything and really want to help you. A lot of people fall in that last category. They don't know something or they are not able to recall something, but they want to help. So without always knowing it, they invent. That can lead to deep inaccuracies. Unless you are extremely careful, extremely scrupulous in using the interview form, you are inviting trouble.

GM: In the end, how did you get at the "true" Hughes, if there is such a thing?

AR: I don't know if I ever did. But by the way, I don't think you can ever get the "truth" of a character, because the character doesn't know his or her own truth. So nobody can say, "This is a true portrait" of the subject. Even in life, you could ask five friends about the true character of a certain person and come up with five different opinions. You will in fact come up with five different opinions. No two people are going to give you identical pictures of this individual. So who's right and who's wrong?

No, I don't think I ever came to the true picture. What I did was to search for the evidence that Hughes left behind in more unguarded moments—for letters, especially early letters of adolescence and young manhood when he wasn't writing for posterity as he was toward the end of his life; and early poetry and prose, which is tremendously important. I was the first person to go to Cleveland, to the Western Reserve Historical Society, and I discovered his high school monthly magazines and saw the kind of poetry he wrote when he first started to write. I saw how at the age of seventeen, eighteen, although he was a jock, a star athlete—the best high jumper in the school, on the relay team—he was writing poetry in which he seemed to be describing himself as a little boy in need of a nurturing mother. That kind of violent paradox tells you a great deal. That's what I looked for. And then, of course, if you're lucky you come across evidence of his attitude in a moment of crisis when he's of a more mature age. In that case, it was finding letters or drafts of letters that he had saved which he had written to God-mother—Mrs. Mason. When she is banishing him from her presence and later, when he is begging to be readmitted, you see a level of inner turmoil, a capacity for self-abasement, which you had never guessed at. Just thinking about that, decades later, made him feel sick. So you fasten on that and try to get some kind of psychological portrait, knowing that you are really stabbing in the dark. I think if you are humble enough, but yet still try, you can achieve something useful, something that coheres with other aspects of the life.

GM: It sounds from what you are saying that his writing in fact gave you quite a bit of insight into Langston Hughes. Do you think that is true only because so much of it is autobiographical? Or do you think that any writer's work reveals something of the life, no matter how "objective" it may seem?

AR: I think the latter, that almost any work by a serious artist, if it's approached carefully, contains evidence of the psychological state and psychological history, too, of the writer. I don't think there's any doubt about that. I say a "serious" writer; I mean a writer who indulges in subjectivity. I don't mean a detective story writer—but even of such a person, you could still read something of his psychological history, I think. In the case of Hughes, I think that is true, especially of the earlier work, as I've said before. That, I think, is particularly revealing. But throughout his life, it's true. On the other hand, I didn't feel that as a biographer I had to be constantly referring to the art; in fact, I felt obliged as a narrator not to let the story become bogged down by analyses of books that the audience had not read.

GM: What was your relationship to the subject? For example, did you identify with him?

AR: As I said, I certainly admired and respected him, but I found that it was very important to keep a distance from

61

him—not to allow him to penetrate my own spirit, not to believe that I had some special relationship to him, that we were kindred minds or kindred spirits, or anything like that. I believe that there was a necessary process when I had to empathize with him, to understand what he was doing, what he was thinking, what he was saying. Beyond that it was just as important to realize that I was not he, and he was not I.

In fact, if I felt myself becoming too close to him, in talking to friends—and I talked all the time about the project to friends because I discovered early on that it was important to do that. It was a source of information and reflection. Anyway, I would talk about him slightingly and call him names like "runt," "pipsqueak," "little son of a bitch" or "bastard"—anything to get distance. Of course, I didn't bring that attitude to the writing, just as I wouldn't write with too much empathy. I was, however, determined to reveal anything bad about Hughes that I discovered. That was one of my early commitments. I would not hide anything about him, even if it might offend some people.

GM: Did spending so much time with Langston Hughes change you in any way?

AR: Living through his life experience intellectually gave me another range of experience, of vicarious experience. I lived through his problems and his adventures; he took me places where I would not have gone ordinarily, like the Soviet Union. I also learned a lot from his commitment to his art and from his commitment to his people. It was instructive reading his work, reading his essays, following his train of thought, his mind and his principles. Yes, they had their effect upon me, the same effect that he hoped his work would have on any reader.

I believed in him at the end. I believed in him in the middle and also at the end. I still believe in him, in what he was trying to say.

GM: Did you have any theories of biography or psychology besides the ones we've touched on that guided you as you tried to interpret his experience?

AR: Theories of biography or psychology?

GM: Yes. It seems to me that whether it's articulated or not, implicit in every decision the biographer makes when he or she tells a life is some sense of what makes life meaningful or what shapes the self.

AR: I can't say that I had any particular psychological theory, though I guess I believe in basic Freudian psychology, especially as developed by, say, Eric Erikson—his theories of identity. I did not go deeply into psychology—only to the extent of believing that the childhood was a most significant arena, or trying to discover basic mental truths about the individual, or supposing that certain conflicts would have their roots in infancy. Now, that I would say is a modest degree of psychologizing, but compared to other biographers, it is a substantial commitment to psychology. I feel sorry for biographers and for the readers of their biographies who do not make a similar commitment, who try to pretend that Freud did not exist or act as though his theories have no validity.

As for theories of biography, I would simply emphasize that biographers should make very modest claims and modest suppositions about what it is they are doing. I think the self cannot be recovered, the truth cannot be recovered, the truth cannot even be identified—not the truth of the life, only certain facts. Basically, biography is the art of approximation. I think it does best when it adheres to very strict standards of verification, without sacrificing the validity of insight—psychological and artistic insight. But it must hold itself to fairly high standards of verification.

GM: Do you think of biography as a genre?

AR: Yes. I'm not sure what that means, but I think it's a genre.

GM: I ask because there are so many different types of biography and so many ways of practicing it. Considering the range of books one might call biography, it sometimes seems to defy classification. It seems a hybrid form.

AR: I'm not sure about that. I think there's much more of a problem with autobiography. I mean, there are straight-forward autobiographies. Then you can talk about fiction as being autobiography and poetry as being autobiography. The whole world becomes an autobiography. By compari-son, biography is much less complicated a subject.

GM: Does the question of whether biography is an art or a craft concern you?

AR: An art or a craft, or an art or a science? Or an art, craft, or science?

GM: Let's consider all three.

AR: All right. I don't think it can be an art in and of itself. In its basic form, I think it is a science. Of course, it's not totally a science—at its best it's a fusion of art and sci-ence. But I would say the more important element is the sci-ence. By that, I mean that what is really crucial is the verification of fact and opinion. One has constantly to offer evidence to support one's opinion. That I judge to be more proper to the scientific than the artistic method.

GM: Did you feel yourself called upon to be creative in any aspect of writing biography?

AR: Yes, yes. I thought the biography had to be well written. A lot of biographies are very badly written. Some of the praised biographies are not very well written. I worked very hard to balance sentences and to structure paragraphs. I tried. I felt it had to be well written. That I think I learned as much as anything from R. W. B. Lewis, who wrote a beautiful biography—as he had to, to match Edith Wharton, because her work is so carefully, so elegantly structured. His work matches hers in the quality of its prose.

As I said before, I wanted to hold the reader's interest, and so I had to structure the story according to chapters so that each moved along. Of course, the life was just packed with interest and fit itself into certain cycles or episodes.

GM: Do you have any rules or advice for those who might want to write biography?

AR: I have no real rules or guidelines. A lot depends on the size of the archive—the amount of material. There are so many variables that it's hard to come up with a set of rules. The first is get hard evidence: What is out there, and what can you recover? If you can't recover a great deal, you can't write the same kind of book that you would write if you had a lot of evidence. Again, I would reiterate what I said before about biography being an art of approximation, not of absolute certainty. I also believe that psychological investigation is very important as opposed to pretending that somehow it's a violation to try to enter the mind of the individual—that is, so long as you do it in a gingerly, respectful fashion. I think that biographies of women and blacks and other minorities and quasi-minorities have to set a lot of the political questions aside and tell the story, and let the political chips fall where they may. If this means taking down the subject a peg or two, so be it. And you need to reveal whatever needs to be revealed.

GM: Was that a problem writing a so-called "official" biography?

AR: No. Volume one appeared without being approved by the executor or trustees.

GM: Did you get any response from them afterwards?

AR: No, because there was still volume two to come. I was fortunate in my executor. He understood the situation, and respected my right to tell the story as I saw fit. I would not want to write a biography that had to be approved at the last minute by an executor.

GM: Are you already thinking about what you will work on next?

AR: No, not really. I think a relevant question is whether I would do another biography. First I said that I would never do another biography, because I can't take out another nine years of my life for one subject. I could not, I think, become a professional biographer. I need to feel a great deal of respect for my subject. That's the only way I got through nine years of Langston Hughes. I continued to respect him, what he stood for, what he hoped to achieve—his lofty sense of purpose. Those things sustained me when I naturally began to flag or falter. But if I found the right person, I would probably do another biography.

GM: Have you given much thought to why there seems to be this "biography boom" in the twentieth century in general and recent years in particular?

AR: I think that people have always been interested in lives, but I guess that our standards have now relaxed so much that we can publish certain things about people that we could not have published before, certainly not in the Victorian age. The individual is not as sacrosanct as he or she once was. Also, publishing has become a juggernaut in the academic world, where a lot of biographies originate. Subjects are being gobbled up left and right. I don't know if there's anything particular about our age that makes biography more interesting to the masses of readers. The opportunity is there for the publisher to make money. I don't think of it as a pernicious thing.

A lot of people buy biographies. I was told by someone in book selling that biographies sell more in hard cover than in paper; that they have a limited sale in paper. I don't know if that's true or not.

GM: Perhaps they are given as gifts.

AR: Possibly they are given as gifts. People perceive them as having a long shelf life; they'll always be there. In any case, I think that a lot of people who buy them never read them. They see them as tombstones. Memorials of people they admire. And because biographies are seen as monumental and tributary, biography therefore has—not a sacredness to it, but inherently a prestige to it that a novel doesn't have.

GM: There does seem to be something permanent about it.

AR: Yes. It's not ephemeral, even though the life itself was more or less ephemeral.

Conversation with

Michael Mott

I had met Michael Mott twice before our conversation about biography, first when he received an honorary degree from Saint Mary's College, Notre Dame, Indiana, where I teach, and again, when he attended a conference there on Thomas Merton. Familiar with *Counting the Grasses,* a collection of Mott's poetry, and with others of his wide-ranging books, I looked forward to *The Seven Mountains of Thomas Merton,* which I read soon after it was published in 1984. His was one of the first names that occurred to me as I made up my list of the biographers with whom I would like to meet.

On a perfect spring day, I drove to Mott's home near the campus of Bowling Green University in Ohio, where he heads the writing program. He led me to a studio in the carriage house behind the main dwelling to meet his wife, Margaret, an artist, who was weaving at her loom. Then Mott and I walked along the brick streets of the historic district in which he lives to downtown Bowling Green, where we had lunch and began our conversation. We finished back at his house, in the high-ceilinged front parlor. He talked fluently, energetically for several hours, his accent unmistakably British, even though he is half American. Afterwards, Amanda (one of the Motts' twin daughters) brewed coffee for everyone, which we drank together as we spoke of mutual friends.

Gail Mandell: This must be a switch for you, being interviewed instead of doing the interviewing.

Michael Mott: Yes. I did about seventy or eighty interviews for the Merton book. It's sad—you get so much information and use so little. But of course all the rest is background; it gives you the authority to say what you do.

We might begin with this: I really had to learn the job of being a biographer. I was very much in awe of the whole thing. Then a friend of mine who was doing some research on the early days of Hemingway in Oak Park told me something that I found more useful than almost anybody else's advice. He said he'd walk through Oak Park and meet people who had known Hemingway in the early days. They would agree to see him and before he'd even ask questions, they would give him their meeting with Hemingway, forty, fifty, sixty years ago. They were all beautifully polished, personal verbal essays. "I'm going to give this to you; I haven't given it to anybody else." They would say, "Hemingway said that, I said this; we talked about that, we talked about this." Usually there were two things about these interviews. One, you discovered this same interview in every book about the young Hemingway—it wasn't exclusive at all. They had forgotten, probably, that they'd told the story already. Two, they'd also spent fifty years polishing it, so that every pause was in the right place. And they really resented it if you interrupted.

This happened to me with a number of people. Very quickly I got into a habit of asking questions after they'd finished, and they'd usually look very nonplused, as though they were thinking, "I've already given you this matchless gem." Then I would know that any book by anybody would have this. Usually when I got back for a second interview, I had information from other people. For example, during the first interview with Dom James, Merton's abbot, he told me; in the second, I had the information to ask him questions.

I had thought in my ignorance when I started in '78–'79 that I would probably have considerable trouble with people in the monastery, who would be very guarded about what they said. Instead of being guarded, they were totally unguarded. They would usually come in, in mid-sentence; and goodness knows how many hours later they would go out. And often I hadn't even tape-recorded them, not expecting much. No, the people I had the most trouble with were the New York publishers, the people who had known Merton in his New York days. They were very generous and all the rest of it, but they were too concerned to produce these wonderfully polished pieces. And they held on to them—you know, "Part of the tradition; you can't knock this." With one of them, I did get into quite a lot of trouble over his statements. He rang me up and said, "What's up? I gave you this wonderful interview. Weren't you keeping notes? Didn't you have a tape recorder? Why did you get it all wrong?" Well, the reason I got it "all wrong" was that when I matched it up with various other things, the interview was a little *too* perfect.

I think it's something that every biographer has to be very careful of, that is, buying the whole of a beautiful, polished story. Especially if the subject of the biography has become—I won't say a cult figure—but someone a great many people admire for a great many reasons, so that people who have met them feel bathed in reflected glory, and they're going to fight for that reflected glory awfully hard.

GM: It's interesting that you had this trouble with the publishers and not with the monks, because one might expect that the monks would want to preserve the legend of Merton, the holy man.

MM: No. I don't think that at all. One of the great things in the tradition of the monasteries is the teasing that goes on. I think that it would be extraordinary to be larger than life to one's fellow monks for twenty-seven years. In a certain sense, I think they have the other side of the balance, which is that it's very hard to believe that the wonderful poem or whatever you have in front of you was written by that "ordinary" person you know. The monks were more anxious to prove that Father Louis—as Merton was officially known after he entered religious life—was just another monk of the monastery. "Oh, yes, I knew Tom very well," and so on. "He'd have a beer down by the lake and so would I." I think they came in more on that level.

GM: What were you hoping to get from the interviews?

MM: Well, all interviewers claim that they're open when they go into an interview. I was hoping to avoid asking too many direct questions, but wanted to open people up to talk on their own. I achieved it in the end, but I found that in the beginning I was asking far too many questions—there was far too much of Michael Mott and far too little of the other person. It took me a little while to sit back and just listen.

One of the difficult things about interviewing in the monastery was that at first I didn't know how they would take it. I think it is very nasty to interview somebody and not to declare that you are taping. So I always had the tape deck out, and then I would say, "Do you mind if I get rid of this? You do realize you're being taped?" Then I would put it out of sight, and we'd talk. Sometimes I'd run out of tape just as they became enormously interesting. But it was much better, certainly, than having this thing sitting there going "tick-tick-tick," and the other person thinking, "Oh, my God, I'd better be careful."

The interview with Father Chrysogonus shows you some of the difficulties. I had an idea that he would be the clue to a lot of the political situations in the monastery, which had obviously arisen between Dom James and Father Louis, and other people as well. It seemed to me that Merton was a terrible politician, whatever else he was; he misjudged all that kind of thing, as he did when he thought they wanted to make him abbot. In the end he was terrified that they would, even though there wasn't the faintest chance of it. It was really quite funny, because he sent out this notice saying that he was not even considering being abbot—even though nobody else was considering him. It was sort of an insulting note, disclaiming himself as abbot. I think it was Dom Flavian who said, "Oh, you've done it now. You've done it now. Such a modest statement! Now everybody will be convinced that you're the perfect one for abbot— disclaiming any talent! Such humility! You're a sure-fire candidate now."

GM: Part of the teasing you spoke of?

MM: Oh, yes, that was the teasing, definitely.

GM: What position in the monastery did Father Chrysogonus hold, to make him so important in judging the politics of the monastery?

MM: He didn't really hold high positions. He's interested in music, so he would be the choirmaster—that sort of thing. I think he was the underprior at one point. But he had been there as long as anybody. For the most part he went his own way, but he was a friend of both Dom James and Father Louis. They would go to him for advice. Certainly, he was one of the main intellectuals in the monastery.

He had joined Merton in the series of lectures that they gave to the novices and professed monks. He is a musicologist and music historian, very well known all over Europe. He's also a scholar of the Trappist order, particularly of La Trappe itself.

I had the feeling that he would probably know what was exaggerated and what was down-to-earth about the political situation at Gethsemani in the fifties and sixties. I hadn't interviewed him the first two or three times I had been at the monastery, but I had written him a note to ask him if he would mind my interviewing him. He said that would be all right. But Brother Patrick Hart and the others said, "He won't give you five minutes. He's withdrawn and guarded. Hates biography—eats it for breakfast." So I didn't even bother with a tape recorder. I thought that would frighten him even more. If I could get even five minutes with him, I thought, I could ask him a couple of questions. Well, he stayed and he stayed. He talked brilliantly and answered all the questions I wanted without my even asking. I refashioned a whole section of the book after I had talked to him, because it made so much better sense. It was a point of emphasis rather than anything else, but it seemed to me much more balanced in judgment. When he went—it must have been about six o'clock—I had to get my notebook out. I missed dinner, I missed everything. I just scrambled the notes down frantically so that I wouldn't leave out anything important.

GM: Were the interviews your most valuable source of insight into Merton?

MM: Yes. Well, that's difficult to say. Certainly in combination with the journals. I was in an enviable position because I did have Merton's own journals. Some of them, anybody could read—the ones at Saint Bonaventure's University in Olean, New York, for example. It was only the journals from the last six or seven years of his life that no one else had access to, but even a good deal of that he had edited and put into *Conjectures of a Guilty Bystander* and other, later books. But still, I had an enormous advantage.

Sometimes, it was a funny advantage. I had read his journals from 1930–40 at Saint Bonaventure's, and I'd then be interviewing an old friend of his, maybe an old girlfriend of his, and she wouldn't know what I knew or didn't know. That made one particular person a good deal more guarded than she otherwise might have been, wondering, "What the heck did Tom Merton say about all that at the time?" Another funny occasion was when I was reading Merton's '38–'39 journal. Robert Lax was at Olean at the time. I had just met Lax, and I remember saying that afternoon, "You had an argument, didn't you, on your birthday, when you came down from Olean to New York City in 1938?" He looked at me. "Merton and I never argued." I said, "All right, I'm sorry." (Lax, you know, is terribly gentle.) I said, "Perhaps not an argument. Merton refers to it as an argument. Maybe he's exaggerating." "Oh," Lax said, "well, he did get a little hot, maybe." You know, to be able to check a diary entry from 1938 with someone then and there—Lax was right there and the diaries were right there. It was just extraordinary.

Robert Lax gave me some details that confirmed my very strong suspicion that Merton had several times in the *Seven Storey Mountain* taken conversations widely apart in time and put them together as one talk. I think tidying up an account of one's own life, one might well do it. But I realized that Merton had combined into one the salient points of two talks, one after he and his friend Dan Walsh had come out of a Maritain talk in the spring of 1938 and the other when Lax came down from Olean in the fall.

This happened a number of times in the *Seven Storey Mountain*—and later. From my interview with Dom James, I realized that there were two interviews at Collegeville,

Minnesota, in 1956, not one, and that the first one was an interview between the psychologist Gregory Zilboorg and Merton. This first interview Merton records in his journal at great length. But Dom James was not present at that. Then later, Zilboorg made a serious mistake, I think, in having a second interview in which he humiliated Merton in front of his abbot. That was the one that Dom James knew about, but I didn't at the time. Merton had burst into tears and kept yelling, "Stalin, Stalin," at Zilboorg. I think I would, too. I mean, I have this private conference with the chap, and I say, "Yes, it's very helpful, and I'm going to mend my ways," and then he uses all the knowledge from that private conference to humiliate me in front of my abbot. Merton knew it was the most damaging ten minutes since he had entered the monastery. Later on, in the 1960s, somebody would write on his behalf and say, "He really ought to go to this conference," or something like that, and Dom James would write back and say, "He's not balanced enough; he might have an emotional explosion." Like any person in power, I suppose Dom James would use what he knew about another's weaknesses, and he'd certainly been a witness to those weaknesses in Merton's case. But Dom James knew nothing about the earlier interview. So here I had all Merton's notes on the earlier interview, and I kept asking Dom James questions about it. He said, "What are you talking about?" I then realized Merton had put down nothing about the second interview, which had hurt so much that he couldn't even write about it. He had, though, written to Naomi Burton Stone after the first interview, saying something like, "Zilboorg's got me all buttoned up. I know exactly what's wrong and I'm putting it right." The minute I knew there were *two* interviews, I was in much better shape.

GM: You speak of the advantages of being Merton's "official" biographer. How were you chosen to write the biography?

75

MM: John Howard Griffin was appointed as the official biographer within a year of Merton's death by the trustees of the Merton legacy. The whole situation had been set up by Merton in '67, a year before he went to the Far East; and by the terms of the trust, only the official biographer was to have access to the restricted journals, and to some other materials—correspondence, things like that. I think in a certain sense, Griffin had been somewhat overpowered by these journals. He spent almost all of his time on them, which was fine, but there's a tremendous amount of other material. At any rate, Griffin had been working away for five to eight years; then he'd become ill.

The trustees were getting anxious about whether the book would be finished. The chief trustee at the time, Naomi Burton Stone, had been Merton's agent and friend for over thirty years. She was asked to do a report, and at that point the publishers came up with my name. They had published *Helmet and Wasps,* a novel of mine, some years before and Robie Macauley, who had recently joined Houghton Mifflin, knew me from our short time working together on the *Kenyon Review.* He wrote to me and asked me if I was interested in Thomas Merton—nothing about biography, as I recall—just was I interested in Thomas Merton? I wrote back and said I was, but presumed hundreds of others were, too.

I had approached Merton from the essays of the sixties backward. I had always been very nervous indeed of *Seven Storey Mountain,* for my own reasons. One was that I had read a book in England by Douglas Hyde called *I Believe.* Douglas Hyde was a member of the Communist Party in England. He converted to Roman Catholicism and wrote this book about his conversion, which I really disliked. As *Punch* said in a rather devastating one-line review, "Douglas Hyde is obviously a chronic believer." He'd previously said that even if all Communists in the world were wrong, Communism was right. Now he was saying that even if all the Roman Catholics and other Christians were wrong, Christianity was right. I thought it was "By their fruits you shall know them"—probably wrong on that one. But at any rate, I hated the cover of *Seven Storey Mountain,* and I just wasn't ready for another conversion story. Also, I was probably a bit nervous for myself, I don't know.

It was almost by accident I began reading Merton. "Day of a Stranger" was the first thing I read, in New Mexico in '67, and I loved it. It was in a copy of the *Hudson Review,* which I had taken to New Mexico because I was doing a children's book on the Albigensian Crusade and there was an article in that number on the Albigensians, the Cathars. I don't remember a word of that article now, but I can remember "Day of a Stranger" almost verbatim.

Back to the letter from Robie asking was I interested in Thomas Merton. One of the things I did after he wrote was to look Merton up in the *Encyclopedia Britannica,* which is a pretty good guide—pretty sexist, considering the number of men compared to women—but a pretty good guide to the general opinion about somebody's importance at any given time. The edition I had came out around 1970, and I found just about two lines on Merton. They talked about him being a monastic reformer, and that was it. I thought, "This is strange." A number of my friends, a very diverse group, were interested in Merton. A Jewish friend of mine was interested in him, and another friend who so far as I know had no religious feeling, but had a terrible mental crisis and then went into Eastern religions, into Zen Buddhism. He said, "Merton saved my mind while I was going through this." I was getting much more interest from the people I knew than the encyclopedia would suggest.

When I went up to Boston to see Little, Brown, who had published a collection of poetry of mine, I told Robie that I would be there, and he said, "Please look in on me at Houghton Mifflin." When I went, I discovered that the Board of Directors were going to take us out to lunch. Not only that, but they wanted to put me up. I was staying with two ex-students of mine in Cambridge; Houghton Mifflin said, "That's ridiculous, you must come and stay in the Parker House." They gave me a suite there. I can tell you this is very unusual treatment for someone who's trying to sell a second collection of poetry. During lunch I was asked whether I was interested in continuing a biography of Thomas Merton by Griffin, and what I would do about it. We discussed this at quite considerable length.

I was very intrigued by the idea, but I was also very worried by it. I thought, "I've never written a biography before. I'll have to learn how to write a biography." Then I was also very worried about picking up someone else's work. I hadn't seen that work at that time, and I didn't know what it was like. Anyway, whose book would it be? Where would my responsibilities begin and end? So I said that I would have to start again from the beginning. They asked how long it would take me if I did have to start from the beginning. I had no way of knowing at that time. They said, "Two years?" In my madness, I said, "Certainly."

Then the other thing I said was that I would like to have a letter from the trustees to cover me at the end. Obviously I could be challenged on questions of fact. Any biographer would expect and want that. But I couldn't be challenged on interpretations of fact. I thought to myself, "Here I'll work away on this thing and at the end of it, each trustee will say, 'Well, this is great, but this has got to be changed, and that has got to be changed,' and we'll end up with a committee book." I had the wit to do that, although I really didn't know what I was doing. The publishers agreed to try to get a letter from the trustees, but they said, "At the same time, we want something from you, Mr. Mott. We want you to write a report on how you would go about writing this biography."

I was asked to give a whole lot of answers before I even knew the questions. I read the *Seven Storey Mountain* and about six other Merton books and thought about it very hard. I spent about three weeks writing the report, which was longer than they'd asked for—it's about fifteen to twenty pages—and I sent it off. It's embarrassing to me now when I read that report, but I really had worked pretty hard on it. Then I heard nothing at all, and I thought, "This is a very polite way of saying, 'You're obviously not the right chap for this.'" Which didn't surprise me. So I went up into the mountains in north Georgia and got on with something else. Then at the end of the summer, I received a letter saying they wanted me to write the biography. In the meantime, I'd got a job as writer-in-residence at the College of William and Mary, where I turned up in the fall of '78. It took me a long time to get into writing biography. Really, '78–'79, I was just going through the usual scares and fears and frights. I was reading a lot of Merton, and by the time the end of that year rolled by, I had read most of his published work. But I hadn't written a line (or whatever lines I had written, I had torn up). I was given a Guggenheim Fellowship for '80, thank goodness, and again most of that time was spent on research. By this time, I was interviewing people and all the rest of it. As we all know, the book took me far longer than two years.

By the fall of '80, I had to find a job. My Guggenheim money was spent; my advance money was spent. I accepted a full professorship at Bowling Green State University, and the actual writing of the book—putting it through three drafts and various other changes—was done with full-time teaching, which meant that every weekend, every summer, every spare minute was taken. By that time the money for the book had run out, of course, and things were becoming very nerve-wracking. Except that I now had a book, which I then worked through again. The drafts were well over a thousand pages. And I was typing them all. Then Amanda, my daughter, and I put the last draft on a word processor. It was a lot of work.

GM: You say you had to learn how to write biography. How did you do that?

MM: Largely by thinking about it, and making the usual false starts. I did have my models, needless to say. Boswell's *Life of Johnson* is the most obvious model. There were other models, with things about them that I liked and things that I disliked.

From trying a few years earlier to write an autobiography that started with my earliest memories and ended when I was thirteen, I realized the whole mythmaking process that we all get into about our own childhood, which keyed me into Merton's approach. You see, one of the things I felt at first was that if I was going to finish the book in two years, all I would need to do was to take Merton's word for the first twenty-seven years of his life. After all, he'd written a very well known autobiography. Then I'd concentrate on the last twenty-seven years of his life, which would be my job. That seemed fine, until I thought about this attempt to write a short autobiography of myself to the age of thirteen. It began to dawn on me that an autobiography and a biography are two very different things, and if you confuse them you're in real trouble. I was lucky. At the same time I was learning from my friend to be a bit skeptical about the prepared statement.

While I was in Williamsburg, I also happened on the correspondence between Owen Merton, Merton's father, Evelyn Scott, and Lola Ridge. Merton and Scott were writing to Ridge, this young poet in New York, about one another. From that correspondence, I got the whole story of the affair between Evelyn Scott and Owen Merton in Bermuda.

When I went up to Boston to look at the typescript of the *Seven Storey Mountain,* I thought, "For goodness sake, Michael, look at the Bermuda account. Merton may have included a lot of things about Bermuda which were taken out." We know that the book went through a number of drafts and deletions. The religious authorities insisted on cuts, the editors cut, Merton cut. Looking through the typescript, I thought there may be a lot of things: A, in the Bermuda section and B, in the Cambridge section. Well, everybody would look in the Cambridge section to find out what dreadful things this young man had been up to, but not the Bermuda section. They would just take that as published—that is, unless they had seen the Owen Merton-Evelyn Scott-Lola Ridge correspondence.

Gradually, I began to feel that *Seven Storey Mountain* left out a lot that was very, very important about this little boy wandering adrift in an arts colony in Bermuda. I began to feel that some of the things that Merton said he felt about his mother weren't really about his mother at all but were about Evelyn Scott—that she'd been the real disciplinarian. Now, clearly Merton had a grudge against his mother, Ruth Merton, but that was in part caused by sibling rivalry. He had been the light of his mother's eye. Every time he turned over in his sleep, she was writing about it. Then John Paul turned up, and his mother—having convinced the child that everything he did was important—turned all the attention off. So it was sibling rivalry of a very special kind. The written record had been broken off, and he'd got to pick the record up as quickly as he could and make it as comprehensive as possible. In a certain sense, all of Merton's writing is a continuation of "Tom's Book," written by his mother in his first and second year. So I had that strong feeling, but I also wondered why Ruth Merton was such a bad thing in his life. All right, she was cold, she was intellectual, she was this, she was that. She was always wandering around looking very concerned, very worried. Well, she had reason to be worried. Her husband couldn't support the family. But there were other things involved. I'd heard that his mother had been such a disciplinarian; I had a feeling that he'd escaped from his mother after her death into the company of his father. His father was always a very beloved figure, but an uncertain entity—very charming and sweet and all the rest of it—but really not very efficient. I have no doubt father and son ate out the whole time they were in France, for example. Everything was rather good fun, but at the same time uncertain and therefore a little anxiety-making.

Then to have the mother replaced by Evelyn Scott! Evelyn Scott's own son Creighton says that when Owen was away trying to sell pictures in New York, there was a huge battle between Evelyn Scott and Tom Merton. I also got the feeling from Evelyn Scott, and to some extent from Owen, in the correspondence, that Tom was a pretty formidable rival at the age of ten. The battle was between Evelyn and Tom, and Evelyn was under no illusions about that. She writes pretty vitriolicly about the ten-year-old boy who was getting between her and Owen. Evelyn comes right out and says, "With Tom there, there was no possibility of getting married." There were many other things as well that I just happened on—clearly Owen told Evelyn an awful lot about the marriage with Ruth. But I wasn't writing the biography of Evelyn Scott or Owen Merton.

Then of course I thought to myself, "What else has been left out of *Seven Storey Mountain* if all of this very important material has been deleted?" I mean, Merton (and it obviously was the author this time) left out Creighton—Tom Merton wasn't wandering around alone in Bermuda, he was wandering around with Creighton. The whole of the Evelyn Scott thing is left out, and it really colors everything. It's not there, but it colors everything, and if you've got something that's not there but colors everything, then you become intrigued.

To be a little briefer than I've been up to this point, I realized that the last thing I could do honestly was to take Merton's word for the first twenty-seven years of his life. Usually for very honorable reasons. He didn't want to blow the whistle on his father, who was always a very complicated figure for him. Owen was a saint, but he was always letting his son down.

This curious wound which Merton's mother had given him, or which Evelyn Scott had given him, lasts right up to the correspondence with Rosemary Reuther in 1967. That quotation I got from the correspondence with Rosemary Reuther, which I use over and over again in the book—it's really devastating, I think.

GM: Which one is that?

MM: "I don't take sweetly to rejection, I can tell you." That's the quotation. It's one of about three key phrases. You know, if you take key phrases, you may be guilty of exaggeration. You have to be very careful about that, because sometimes they bolster up some theory of yours which may or may not be right, but I thought "I don't take sweetly to rejection" was really important.

I also went back to *Seven Storey Mountain* to a line where Merton's talking about one of the trips he took as a teenager from New York back to London, and he says, "I had easily acquired a very lurid reputation for myself with scarcely any trouble at all." This seemed to apply to a number of incidents in his life, not just when he was a student, but much later. He couldn't resist the glib remark, which didn't have much to do with reality but fed the other person's impression of him. You know, something like, "All right, you think I'm a bad person. I'll really give you some ammunition."

Again, I was proofreading my text in the book against the journals when I came to that remark made when Dom James called him in, in the middle of the affair with "S," the young nurse Merton fell in love with while he was a monk; this is in Merton's restricted journal. Merton is parting from Dom James and says, "When the child is born, you can be its godfather." I mean! I said to myself, "There's not going to be any child, and this is just smart aleck talk to ginger up Dom James." In the same interview, this time according to Dom James, Dom James said, "Well, you'll probably be leaving the monastery to marry her." Why, no! That wasn't his plan. But like many of us he was probably working out six plans at the same time. To have Dom James assume that he was going to leave the monastery to marry "S" changed his attitude. After that, Dom James said to me, "I got a very different impression of this affair," and so would I have done. So would anybody, I think. But that remark, "You can be its godfather!" Then Merton goes on in the journal, "But we are a pair of damned cats." That made me look again at things that people had assumed, thinking they had got just the tip of the iceberg because all the rest had been cut away by censors and others. Maybe those things were there and maybe they weren't.

In another interview Lax said to me, "Oh, yes, I knew all about Merton before I met him. He was something of a hero among his fraternity brothers because he had to leave Cambridge because of an illegitimate child and probably two. He would have been tarred and feathered and run out of town on a rail if he hadn't left." So Lax told me he had heard all about that. I had an idea that Lax was sort of smiling over it, as if it might be true and it might not be true. There are ways of spreading rumors by trying half a sentence and quitting on it. You don't have to produce an outright lie. Heaven knows, in a certain sense I've done that, too. Then you can get mad at people later on because they've built on what you half said or only implied, though you probably intended they should build on it. If they don't build on it, you have to give them another bit of the sentence.

But going back to that line in the *Seven Storey Mountain,* "I had easily acquired a very lurid reputation for myself with scarcely any trouble at all," you could play that off an awful lot of incidents in Merton's life. Again, in meeting Ginny Burton, I realized that neither Lax nor Ginny Burton really thought that Merton was a tremendous womanizer. I thought, "Well, if his best friend—Lax was his best friend—and his girlfriend at that time didn't think he was such a womanizer, then . . ." On the other hand, his other great friend Ed Rice was sure Merton had been seeing a lot of women. But Merton could have been feeding him all kinds of stuff, for all I know. Best to take it with a grain of salt, as I think Ginny Burton did, too. It's difficult to get to the truth in these matters. Once you've begun to see passages like that, however, and to play them against the text, you become a bit more skeptical.

GM: In spite of the difficulty of interpretation, would you say that an autobiography is the best basis for a biography?

MM: Absolutely. Especially when in addition to the autobiography, you have all the journals—wonderful journals. Coming back to what I was trying to say before, you certainly do realize the difference between biography and autobiography in working with both. You realize that a biographer has certain duties and a different approach to the subject than an autobiographer. When I was writing my autobiography to the age of thirteen, and I showed it to my mother, she would say at times, "Oh, you got that completely wrong. It wasn't that way at all. You'll have to change that." I would say, "I'm not going to change that. In the first place, *you* could be wrong, too. Why should I take your word for it? And in the second place, it doesn't really matter how I got that impression, what's important is the impression—you know, the coloring." I suppose if I realized I got something wrong in an autobiography, I would put in a footnote to say I was basing that assumption on the wrong knowledge. I made a mistake, but what I did with that mistake is the important thing.

But in biography as opposed to autobiography, if you come upon a situation like the one described earlier, where plainly your subject got the wrong end of the stick or made a bad guess on wrong information, you have an obligation to report that. The main thing in biography is still the decision that they made, the judgment they made, and what they did with it.

GM: It sounds like a daunting task to try to make sense of so many disparate sources of information and various points of view, both in the writings of Merton himself and also in all the interviews. When did you—if you ever did—really feel you "had" Merton? Was there a moment when you finally felt you understood him?

MM: No, oh no. That's a difficult question to answer, but the only honest way of answering it is "no." I think I know Thomas Merton much better than most of the people with whom I've spent my life because I haven't made a study of them for six years. There certainly are points beyond which one could not pretend to know—certainly that's the case with a volatile character like Merton, always changing and always trying new things. In a negative way, I think it helped my own confidence in knowing when not to trust information, and also knowing, as I say in the preface to the book, that Merton was an honest person—but even an honest person can entertain and create false ideas about themselves. And Merton was very good at creating false ideas about himself. I had to be really careful. For example, take the question of whether he was going to go back to Gethsemani after he left Bangkok. He might meet somebody casually, waiting for a plane in northern India, and within a half an hour he'd go over that with them. He'd bounce the idea off them: "You think I should spend the rest of my life in that monastery?" Needless to say, they'd get the impression that he wasn't going to go back there. Meanwhile, he might be writing to Dom Flavian saying that he was going to come back there, but he wanted to see Wales first, he wanted to see Ireland first, he wanted to see this, that, and the other. The impression was he'd roll into Gethsemani about 1989. I had to be very careful not to fall into the same wrong impressions that these people had. This was just the way Merton talked. I wasn't so sure that all those people he talked that way to shaped Merton's life, even though he might have made them feel they had. He was very good at playing ideas off against a person, then making up his own mind which way he was going.

Dom James was the wall he bounced his ball off for years. Merton realized the importance of that, and when Dom James retired as abbot, he went looking for a substitute for Dom James. He found him in the Archbishop of Louisville, who told him, "No, I don't think you ought to be out of the monastery more than twice a year." He'd been out once already in 1968 and he figures the year's almost finished, so he then starts expanding his second trip outward, to include New Mexico, Alaska, India, Sri Lanka, Thailand, Indonesia, Malaysia, Hong Kong. . . .

GM: He sounds like quite a character to have to interpret—full of contradictions.

MM: Everybody said there was something of a barrackroom lawyer in Merton. In the early days, he would ask, "Can I do this?" And the answer would come back, "Yes, you can." "Well, can I do this on all possible occasions?"

GM: Was there some central or unifying factor in him? Some core that held him together, made him coherent?

MM: I think so. But no one will ever know the complete answer to that question—I'll never know the answer to that question in total. Certainly the central concern of Thomas Merton's life was to know God. It doesn't change, and it was always there, dormant perhaps. It doesn't really change from the time of his conversion. Other things have to shape themselves around that concern in one way or the other.

There is also a fascination with himself and therefore a tendency not only to self-consciousness but to playing and watching the play at the same time. He knew that perfectly well. And he knew that it made him phony to himself on a certain plane. It was getting at that phoniness that was difficult. It's not a good thing for a poet, or for a monk, I would suggest, or for anyone else. One of the monks said Merton cautioned him as a novice against watching himself pray and saying, "Here am I praying," and the monk said, "I never had that problem until he introduced me to it." Then after that, he had the problem.

GM: What did you learn about Merton that surprised you the most?

MM: I keep being surprised. I'm perfectly capable of being surprised right now. And that really says something enormous about somebody one has studied for over six years. What surprised me the most? The range of the man is just extraordinary. I think the very fact that I can't think of one thing suggests that in writing this biography I was determined to, as it were, put the reader in the same situation I had been in. That is, to amass the material, to present it in the best possible way, then let the reader decide. To let the reader be surprised! To leave the great theories out. Some of the critics asked why I hadn't included another twenty pages at the end on Thomas Merton's place in the Catholic Church twenty years after. There was a very good reason for that—I'm totally incompetent to do that; that would take another six years, maybe.

Anyway, unlike some biographers, I'm not a "pattern" man, one who finds a pattern and then looks at everything in terms of this. When I was writing my autobiography to the age of thirteen, someone asked, "Are you going to give a

Jungian interpretation, an Adlerian interpretation, a Freudian interpretation?" I wanted to finish it and then let people see any patterns afterward. This is very much my way of doing biography, too. It's empirical. If something turns up that I've got to include, too bad about any preconceived pattern or anything else.

Having said that, there are certain things that I thought I saw early on, such as this idea seeded in Merton so early on—his own importance. Somebody sitting there staring at you all the time and writing everything down would tend to give you that impression. Quite unlike our house when I was growing up, where you learned you weren't all that important. Nevertheless, there is a parallel with Merton: I kept journals from the age of twenty-one. Personally, I think Merton found himself of incredible interest. There was a fascination with himself. With Merton, almost everything, no matter what it might be, is autobiographical, or potential food for autobiography. For me, the purpose of my journal is in a way to get all that stuff out of the way before I start writing about someone else or something else. All writing is self-revealing—you can't deny that—but I don't write an essay, shall we say, on some controversy or other and include pages of autobiography, which he does at times.

GM: I think for many readers the episode with the young nurse, "S," which you referred to earlier, was the biggest surprise. Was that episode in character or not?

MM: Merton saw it in character himself, and he didn't want it left out of the picture of his life. I knew about it very early on in writing the biography. In fact, there were so many rumors around that people would come up to me and say, "How are you going to deal with that?" Griffin had written that whole part straightaway, and I think he had blown it out of all proportion. I think he had asked himself the question, "What am I going to do about that?" and explaining it had become an absorbing interest. I did want to try to see the relationship in a balanced way and neither write it down nor write it up. I also wanted to try to see things from her point of view.

GM: Did you have the chance to interview her?

MM: I talked to her on the telephone. I was going to interview her and she rang up and called it off, saying it would be too difficult with the family. We talked on the telephone instead. I also had some help from her letters to other people. Her letters to Merton had all been destroyed, and his to her. But there were letters to other people that show how difficult her position was at the time. I have a great deal of respect for her and tried to show understanding.

GM: I wonder whether you think there is a clear pattern of growth and development in Merton. In particular, whether the monastic environment hindered or contributed to his development?

MM: In answer to the first question, yes. He was a very fast-growing person. Dom John Eudes Bamberger said he was a good self-corrector, and I think he was. But that's difficult. It doesn't account for all the damage you do. In 1956 Merton was overzealous in trying to cure his poor novices of everything by using psychoanalysis. He had no qualifications at all for doing that. Finally he realized he shouldn't do it. Well, great. So the doctor's cured, but what about the patient? There was something of that. As Merton says later on, "We must keep moving."

But he did grow, and his growing pains were suffered not only by himself but by everybody around him. In a confined area like a monastery, that was kind of tough on the other monks. Also, his ambiguities about himself were tough on the other monks. I try to point that out. All right, in 1965 he's finally given a hermitage; everyone wishes him the very best—they write him farewell cards—and he goes off to the woods. And then, he blames them for leaving him alone! I don't know how you solve that problem. Many of us feel that way. We want solitude, but we also want company in our solitude.

GM: How would a man so self-reflective miss the implications of his behavior?

MM: What's clear from the inside may not be from the outside, and vice versa. In the monastic situation, you may see slights where none exist. A glance or lack of a glance can build up inside you for weeks, I suppose. Even saying all that, he did have blind spots, for example, regarding his need for travel. He loved to travel. He was always making up excuses why he had to be here or there. One of the surprises—you asked me earlier about surprises—is to find a man, who was so remarkably clear-sighted, blind in certain spots. But to me, the most important thing (because we're all blind in spots) is that in "Hagia Sophia" he really does begin to explore not only his own blindness (what he's been blind to) but the blindness of others (what they have been blind to). Through that exploration, he begins to see what has been left out in certain situations. This to me is the big liberating process. He opened out to everything, and all at the same time. "We've neglected women, and what else have we neglected?" he asks. We've neglected this, we've neglected that. His discoveries were amazingly significant, and not only for himself, of course. He begins to speak for others.

GM: But the monastery seems like such a strange choice for him: here was a man who loved to travel but took a vow of stability; he loved to talk and to write and took a vow of silence. Was it productive for him to go against his own grain like that?

MM: What is the ideal state for a writer? Is it the university? Most of us there would deny that. Where do you go? When his publisher friend James Laughlin comes down and they're having a picnic, they talk the whole time about poets going mad—Delmore Schwartz was one—and Merton must have come to the conclusion pretty fast, "Aren't I lucky to be protected in this monastery?" I think this is a debate most of us have. "Am I better in South Bend or am I better in New York? Maybe I'll get my work published in New York, but I won't have the money to live, and I'll be so overstimulated and distracted I'll do no real work." I think Merton felt constrained in the monastery, but it was a constraint that was also a safety device. Maybe there's something a little childish about that, as Merton saw. He also had temper tantrums when they didn't restrain him enough. But on the whole he dealt with those contradictions awfully well. That's worth recording.

GM: Do you think that in the end he took responsibility for himself and his life?

MM: Yes, I think he did. He did. He uses the word "infantile" very strongly in the midsixties, for example, when he's talking about white liberals patronizing blacks, treating them as children, taking over their movement or trying to. He has a wonderful phrase, "incurable infant." He talks about "incurable infant" attitudes in the monastery. That reflects back on himself: "Am I an incurable infant?" One thinks back to the first Zilboorg interview when he tried to deal with that. I think Merton discovered the balance between the need for protection and responsible freedom—a Zen koan and a Christian paradox.

GM: You're not a Roman Catholic yourself?

MM: No. I'm not a Catholic, but Anglican.

GM: Was it a problem writing the biography of someone not only a Roman Catholic but a Trappist monk?

MM: Being a Roman Catholic might have made things easier—who knows? But I did have a pretty good idea of other things in Merton's experience, some of the things that he revolted against; for example, the sermon at Oakham on the text from Saint Paul is exactly the same sort of sermon I heard at my school thirty or so miles away.

No, I don't think it was a disadvantage, not being Roman Catholic. The only place where it might have been was on the subject of pre-Vatican and post-Vatican II, and I did try to inform myself pretty well on that. Other things, like the battle over the liturgy—well, we have our battles over the liturgy. So far, nobody has said to me, "Too bad, you got that all wrong. Too bad you aren't Roman Catholic."

One of the things I decided on the very day I had lunch with the publishers was that I was going to keep my own counsel while I was writing the biography, and I was going to be very, very, very careful about associating myself with *any* group. One of the things I learned about Merton is not just that he is controversial but everyone has a vested interest in him in some strange way. I've had people say, "I thought your book was all right, but your Merton isn't my Merton, and my Merton is this. . . ." I'm very willing to hear that, but I do hope I've managed to incorporate a number of the many Mertons in this book—otherwise it's really too bad.

GM: You say in the preface that you never met Merton. Was that a serious disadvantage?

MM: We'll never know. I would like to meet him now. I feel I came close to meeting Merton in spending a good deal of time with his friends. It's a pity I couldn't consult him sometimes. Once, when I was talking to Lax, Lax said he wished he could just talk to Merton—just call him up. Where was he when he needed him? I felt that way sometimes.

Other things, I think, were very advantageous. I think it was advantageous the book took me so long. I think the timing was right—just about long enough from his death. If I tried to write that book now, too many of the people whom I would want to talk to would be gone. I had almost every possible advantage.

GM: What is it like to live with the idea of someone that long? Did you like him at the end?

MM: Did I like him? Yes. I really did begin to feel he was somebody I knew quite well. But I liked him in the same way you can like a very good friend and yet find some of their traits tiresome. I don't think I idolized him. At the same time, I do like him but find things about him very tiresome. (What he would think of me is another matter!)

GM: About the form you chose for the biography: it strikes me that one of the main unifying factors in this biography is geography—the use of places. How and when did you decide on that?

MM: I guess I was fairly well along on the book when I got to that passage in Ruth Merton's letter, which I quote: ". . . it seems to me there is no more fascinating subject in the world than the influence of surroundings on human character." There, certain sparks flew. Place has always been important to me. Often in writing this biography of Merton, I could see things that interest me excessively present in him. I'm not as obsessed about places as he was, but I am obsessed enough about places to realize what he felt. We both lay claim to feelings of restlessness, and ambiguity of place. Incidentally, there's a wonderful way of escaping if one is an alien or a refugee. If you get fed up with the people around you, you retreat into that. So if the people in my American school were rough on me, I became terribly English, and if the English were rough, I became American. Merton was sometimes an advanced case of that.

GM: When you wrote, did you compose in the published sequence?

MM: Yes. Starting with the preface. Absolutely. Starting with waiting for the funeral.

GM: Why did you open the first chapter in 1961, with his visit with Aunt Kit, whom he hardly knew?

MM: Since he and his Aunt Kit were talking about family, it seemed a good place to start. When I tried to write my own autobiography, it was very difficult to sort out what I remembered from what I thought I remembered because I'd been told about it, or from poring over the family album. In fact just this summer I wrote another autobiographical essay, and I started out with something I was told about my birth at the maternity hospital. This conversation with Aunt Kit tied into something like that in Merton's case. If you get the idea from such discussions that you're Welsh, and your mother's name is Welsh, and your father's name is Welsh, and all your life people talk about your "Welsh temperament," even though you have to go a long way back in fact to find anybody in the family who lived there, you find yourself *inventing* a Wales for yourself, as Merton did. The whole first part of *Lograire* is about *his* Wales. He talks about Dylan Thomas and David Jones, people like that with a sort of borrowed affinity. "We Welsh." My own borrowed affinity is Celtic, too, Cornish.

GM: It sounds as though there are many areas of identification between you and Merton.

MM: But I don't think you can lean on that, even though I did recognize it. Maybe Robie thought of that. I never had an education in French schools, but I had an education in English and American ones. That bit about the mores in different schools in different countries fascinated me, though I really didn't think about it until I started trying to write the biography.

GM: One of the questions I always have about somebody like Merton who wrote so much is what sort of problems you had integrating the writings in an account of a life, which is so much more. Was it difficult for you to do?

MM: I don't know about difficult. It did mean that I had to work a lot harder. Upstairs, in my study, I've got ten cases, ten boxes of Merton material—books and copies of the notebooks and all that stuff. You have to assimilate. Then you have to boil it all down. You have to decide what you've got to get in, and what you haven't got to get in. You need to introduce the quotations in some order and in the right places; otherwise, it's just a muddle. Or the other temptation is just to let Merton talk for himself. If we let Merton talk for himself entirely, we're right back to *Seven Storey Mountain.* Keeping that particular balance between interpretation and commentary I think requires only that you know it. As when you're teaching, you have to avoid the great tendency to give it all to your students, all at once, and let them sort it out. There's a point where you've got too little and a point where you've got too much.

Thinking of Alexis De Tocqueville's *L'Ancien régime et la révolution,* you might say there are two great categories: the archivist and the essayist. The archivist has all the materials and the essayist writes great theories and perhaps achieves literature. The biographer tries to combine both, like De Tocqueville. So when you come to write a chapter, the conclusions are drawn from a great deal of work and planning, but you should use the research to say something important, and say it well.

GM: So would that be your model of a good biography—one that achieves these categories?

MM: Oh, yes, I think it's got to do both. It's got to read well, and it has to be reinforced by research.

Above all, I think the whole thing depends on a certain magical distance—that magical distance any portrait painter strives for. If you're too close, a lot of things get blurred. If you're too distant, well, what's the point of the thing, anyway? That's very difficult, finding the right distance.

In a way we're all trying to find the magic distance. We're all trying to get out of solipsism. If you see yourself as the center of the universe, then you're blind to yourself as well as everything else, it seems to me. Yet very few of us can practice detachment, sufficient detachment to see things in focus, not the detachment of indifference.

GM: From what you've said, it seems that the biographer must practice detachment even while being extremely intimate with his subject.

MM: Yes, and the difficulty is certainly compounded if you're dealing with a subject who has himself or herself spent a lifetime puzzling over themselves. As I say, Merton's treatment of his own life is very personal.

GM: Now, you're a poet primarily. Is the kind of creativity you express through writing biography at all similar to that involved in writing poetry?

MM: I don't know, and I deliberately don't know—can you deliberately not know? But these are questions I don't ask myself. I write what I enjoy writing. I write children's books, and I write poetry, and I write novels. Now I've written a biography. I don't consciously take up a different attitude, although I think that each kind of writing helps the others. I know that trying to write a series of novels with a seventeenth-century setting helped my writing of poetry wonderfully, in developing long lines and things like that. But I don't know. Writing the biography certainly put off my writing of poetry and other work. I published one collection of poetry in six years, but that was all, while I was writing the biography.

GM: Do you plan to write another biography, or is Merton an "only child"?

MM: That's an interesting question. After I finished *The Seven Mountains of Thomas Merton,* the publishers asked, "Who are you going to write about now?" And the answer to that was, "Certainly no more about Merton." But the problem was that I couldn't think of anybody else who is as intriguing as Thomas Merton.

Conversation with

Phyllis Rose

Thanks to her clear directions, I found Phyllis Rose's green-shuttered, white clapboard house with no difficulty. It sits at one edge of the campus of Connecticut Wesleyan University, where she teaches English. A steep flight of stairs ascends immediately inside the front door, but to the right, large rooms open one into another: a good house for get-togethers. Rose, accompanied by her dog, Shaemus, led me to the kitchen, where she made tea while we got acquainted. I recognized Shaemus from Rose's series of essays in the "Hers" column of *The New York Times.* She warned me that we might be interrupted by the telephone, because she was waiting for a call from her son, Teddy, also familiar to me from the column.

In fact, because of those essays I had read *Woman of Letters: A Life of Virginia Woolf* and *Parallel Lives: Five Victorian Marriages,* which I then used as texts in various seminars. In person, Rose was smaller than I had imagined—small-boned and fine-featured, with masses of pale hair. We sat in a room just off the entrance hall, at a table that had once been a spool for cable. Rose soon moved aside a large succulent of some sort, profuse with flowers, so that we could see each other better. Even though it quickly became dark outside, the house stayed bright, as lamplight glinted off bare floorboards and caught the colors in exotic rugs and pillows. Shaemus snoozed beside us much of the time, undisturbed by our animated exchange.

Gail Mandell: The first thing I want to ask you about is something you wrote to me when we were arranging this interview. Why have you decided not to talk about biography in public anymore?

Phyllis Rose: It really wasn't as portentous a decision as it may have sounded in the letter.

GM: It sounds as though you had a horrible experience.

PR: Oh, no. I did have a horrible experience, but it didn't have anything to do with biography. It had to do with panel discussions, which I basically don't like. Also, you can spend your life being a professional biographer who talks about biography. I don't want to do that. Also part of me doesn't really consider myself a biographer. Part of me thinks biographers are the kind of people who go down to the county hall and get marriage records and dig and dig and dig and unearth long-lost relatives. Although I wouldn't want to write that kind of book, or at any rate, wouldn't write that kind of book, I feel they are more truly biographers than I am. In that sense, I feel that I'm not qualified to talk about biography publicly. *You* know what kind of biographer I am, so if you want to hear what I have to say, I'm perfectly happy to tell you. But in public, I think that most people assume biography is something other than what I do, and I'm not ready to take on myself the weight of explanation for the kind of biography that I do. I've found that if I'm in a bunch of biographers and they all are, you know, objective, factual biographers, if I really say what I think about biography, I sound like a flake, and I don't want to sound flaky. Essentially, that's why I don't want to talk about biography in public anymore.

I guess there is something there—a serious inhibition, having to do with the kind of biography that I think of myself as doing and my understanding of what biography is seen to be by most people. Because I think most people think of a biographer as somebody who accumulates facts about people's lives. I think of myself as somebody who puts the facts of people's lives into different contexts. Or emphasizes shape somehow and puts facts into new structures. For example, in *Parallel Lives,* there's nothing really very new in that book, yet I hope that the book as a whole is new because of the context in which I've put those rather well-known stories. Very few people know all five of them, or have thought of them in exactly the way I do. I didn't have to do any archival research; I didn't have to discover new letters to do the book.

GM: What attracted you to biographical writing?

PR: Well, I really backed into it, I must say, because I was doing a book about Virginia Woolf, and I was interested in the connections between her life and work. But I thought of that as critical writing, a variation on the sort of literary criticism that I had been taught to do in graduate school. I don't know how I got the idea of putting together the chapters of the books essentially biographically, but I did, and that was a key decision. The biographical parts of that book—especially some of the early chapters—I thought of as necessary to get to what was really interesting, which was the biographical literary criticism later in the book. I had to build up her sense of herself as a woman and the fact that being a woman was important to the way she thought about her life, and so on. But I just thought about that as sitting down and typing, I didn't really think of that as hard

101

to do, and it was the later part that I thought of as key to the book. Then, lo and behold!, I decided to call it a biography (a life, not *the* life—I was careful about that), and people believed that it was.

GM: That's either a testament to your authority or the fluid nature of biography!

PR: Or to people's suggestibility. But when I started doing biography, it was like body surfing. You get on a wave, and you say, "Hey, this really feels good. This is terrific." Suddenly I felt, "I can do this! It's so much fun! Here's a good way of getting at things. It makes material so human, and it gives access of a sort to people who wouldn't ordinarily read this." I just loved it. I thought it was the greatest discovery. I became a proselytizer for biography as a way of doing scholarly writing, because I think that scholarly writing needs some renovation and recasting, which biography offers.

GM: Was it difficult to fuse the biographical and critical writing in *Woman of Letters*?

PR: I still think that it breaks down too much. Ideally, I would not have wanted to write a book in which there were separate chapters on the works. But it began with those chapters. It began first with the chapter on *To the Lighthouse*. I saw ways in which I could read that book that nobody had before because I made connections with her life that nobody had made. Then I did the same thing for *Mrs. Dalloway*. I thought that there had to be a biographical context for this book, too.

It's not ideal. It's not as well integrated as I think a book should be. It's the best I could do at that time. As I say, it was amazing to me, because I was fairly young, to find that kind of criticism acceptable, because it was exactly what I was interested in: the connection between the life and works. It was not critical orthodoxy in the best graduate schools. In fact, it was distinctly unfashionable for many years, and you can't learn it at graduate school. It was something that I just worked out by myself. Still, the structure is life, work, life, work, and I tend to wish I could have integrated it, but I'm not sure if I tried to do it tomorrow, I could do any better.

GM: A few years ago, you made an interesting observation—that you saw biography and fiction moving closer and closer to one another. You wrote that in the future, practice would be the only thing that would separate them, not anything theoretical. Do you still see biography headed in the direction of fiction?

PR: A lot of what I said at that point was based on Mailer's *Executioner's Song.* As it turned out, *Executioner's Song* has not been followed up by anything else. So I'm not sure I was right. They don't seem to be merging. Do you know the books of Collier and Horowitz? They're doing a series of books about American families of power; *The Fords* is one of the most recent, and *The Rockefellers.* The one I read was *The Kennedys,* and it was just an extraordinary book, and there, there's no fictional influence, whatsoever. But it is quite innovative. There are other ways of being innovative in biography besides employing fictional techniques, and when I wrote "Fact and Fiction in Biography," I didn't see that.

GM: Can you say more about your idea of biography and yourself as a biographer?

PR: Well, I'm a relativist. That I think is the big dividing line in biographers. There are biographers who believe, who really believe that you can know absolutely what happened, and there are biographers who don't. And I belong to the biographers who believe that you can't know absolutely and finally what happened. The kinds of things that I'm interested in knowing are things that even the people concerned themselves don't always know. I mean really, really deep structures, really, really deep assumptions. The kinds of situations where everybody disagrees, and nobody knows. I'm not interested in the date of the marriage, the date of the first date, stuff like that which can be known. There are other biographers whom I respect very much, like Robert Caro, for example, who did the Lyndon Johnson biography, who has heard me talk and has said, "I'm really disappointed in you. I didn't think you were one of those fuzzy-minded academics." Caro comes out of a different, a journalistic tradition in which truth can be absolutely established. I come out of an intellectual tradition which doesn't believe in that. I don't know what the sources of it are, but when I teach biography—in fact, when I teach nonfiction writing of any kind—I have my students read a piece by Edward Hallett Carr called "What Is a Fact?" It's a very anthologized piece in which he (we would now say) deconstructs the idea of a fact and tends to turn most facts into opinions. That's what I believe. That's the way my mind was trained to see things. So naturally, the kinds of books that I write don't tend to be accumulations of facts.

What I'm interested in, I would say, is ideology, structure, the way that people's personal frameworks for understanding make their lives turn out the way they have. It's not so much the fact that there's a blurring between fiction and biography or anything, it's just that what I'm concerned with in biography is somewhat different from that other tradition of biographers.

GM: That makes your position clearer. I had wondered from what you wrote whether you thought a biographer might be free to invent so long as the reader were not alienated by the invention.

PR: If you mean invent dialogue, stuff like that, I would never do that. I think it's tacky. I love dialogue. If I can find a recorded dialogue somehow, I'll use it. But I won't invent one. The furthest I would go is, let's say in my new book I have the German director Max Reinhardt trying to persuade Josephine Baker to stay in Germany and train as a serious actress rather than continuing to be a dancer. I put in his mouth some of the things that she said he said. But I also put in his mouth some things that he had said in other interviews, that bore on the situation, that had to do with his feelings about American vaudeville as a source of renewal for European culture. I represented him as saying them directly to her rather than to someone else. But I don't consider that invention. I would never invent an episode or invent a conversation. That seems to me invention in a bad sense.

GM: But you would approve of using fictional techniques—something like flashbacks, for example—so that you're not bound by chronology?

PR: Yes, that's definitely a possibility. Or point of view, very much so, as in the Virginia Woolf book where I narrate her death from the point of view of the cook. For me, it was a way of getting out of a psychological box: I identified with her and she was terribly depressed, in fact suicidal, and I just couldn't write at all, until I figured out this way of breaking out of that identification, which was to identify with the cook instead. I just looked on from a distance. So yes, definitely, techniques like point of view and shift of chronology that you associate with fiction I definitely think are appropriate in biography, but not invention.

105

GM: In *Writing of Women,* you speak of this as a "golden age" of biography, a time when writing and reading lives has come into its own. Why do you think that is?

PR: Why is it happening now?

GM: Yes, why at this time?

PR: I think it's because of the women's movement. Somehow all the political upheaval of the sixties produced this new wave of feminism, and I think that reordered people's sense of what's important in life and what can be written about. Just the very fact that there are lots of biographies being written about women to me means that things are shifting. It isn't just predictable people validated for biography that are being written about now. Everything's up for grabs.

GM: As you pointed out in the same article, Samuel Johnson encouraged others to write the lives of the obscure several centuries ago. Do you think then that it was the women's movement that pushed us to the point where we can now do that, not just think about doing it?

PR: Yes! The other thing I said in that piece is that once you start doing it, then the people aren't so obscure anymore. It's part of a change in what you think of as major and minor, important or unimportant. Johnson wanted to do it, and he wrote about Savage, so Savage is now remembered. He's remembered essentially for nothing except having been the subject of a biography by Samuel Johnson. It's that paradox: if you write about somebody, then they're no longer obscure.

GM: You speak of the way that biography and feminism have vitalized each other, yet I wonder whether a feminist might find biographical writing particularly frustrating. As Jean Strouse has said, there are usually so few female perspectives to draw on, so far as sources of information go. I wonder if you found that problematic in doing either *Woman of Letters* or *Parallel Lives,* having for example to draw on Quentin Bell's life or Leonard Woolf's writings in the case of Woolf, or on various male interpretations of George Eliot or other women in *Parallel Lives?*

PR: Problematic?

GM: Yes, because you then had to sort out the experience of these women as presented or interpreted by males.

PR: Of course, I wasn't just using Quentin Bell's biography of Woolf. I was using her own writings primarily. Actually, I couldn't understand—I was working on my book before Quentin Bell published his book—and I couldn't understand when his book came out how it was he missed this obvious thing that I was going to write about, and I was so terribly relieved because I wanted to be able to write my book. It didn't dawn on me—we were so naive, I think, in some ways in 1972—it didn't dawn on me that because he was a man he simply wouldn't see the same thing in her life that I was seeing. So I've always been grateful that he didn't steal my thunder. But I wasn't getting it filtered through him. That wasn't a problem at all. I was reading her work for myself, and saw stuff in it that was different from what he saw. But it took years to see why he didn't see what I saw.

A good example of the absence of the woman's perspective was in *Parallel Lives,* when I was trying to find material about Catherine Dickens. She just isn't there in the early part. That was where I particularly wanted, as it were, to flesh her out, though God knows she got fleshed out enough later! In the early years, she's only there in references very much by the bye in Dickens' letters. And then there's her daughter's stuff about her. Her daughter was very unsympathetic towards her at first, and she had to be persuaded to a different point of view by George Bernard Shaw, who said, "You can actually be sympathetic towards your mother and think that your father acted like a heel." That was a surprise to Kate Dickens. She would have burned her mother's letters if she had not been taught to see them differently by Shaw.

So first of all, yes, it's true that there's no woman's point of view or even if there was a woman's point of view, as with Kate Dickens, the daughter, it could be essentially male-oriented. Sometimes there are women looking on, but they see through the eyes of unenlightened men, as Dickens' daughter did before another man, Shaw, taught her better. But it is very, very hard to find certain kinds of information.

GM: And did you find that a problem in writing *Parallel Lives?* Was there a difference between writing the men's stories and the women's?

PR: Yes, yes. It's much, much easier to document the men's. Of course, not with George Eliot. But the only case in which I really had problems was with Catherine Dickens. Jane Carlyle was a writer and spoke for herself. And Harriet Taylor: there's enough there. Also, she was documented by Mill. Effie Ruskin had her own letters; there are a lot of letters from Effie Ruskin that have survived and been published. So the only one that really didn't exist in terms of documents was Catherine Dickens. That was the real challenge.

GM: I'm curious about the way you put *Parallel Lives* together, with the double chapters on each marriage, and then the framework of the Carlyles, with at the end the political anecdote used to illuminate the politics of marriage. When did you decide on that structure, and how did you come up with it?

PR: I'm so glad you asked that. I love talking about it. It's the jigsaw puzzle aspect of book writing that I really like—that's when you're writing a book and not just writing an essay or a long monograph, when you have pieces that you can juggle around and put in different kinds of way.

Originally I had the idea of writing about six couples, just because I liked the sound of "Six Victorian. . . ," nothing more important than that. I had to pick a number, and I liked "Six Victorian Marriages," because of the sound. The Darwins were supposed to be the sixth. When I got to the fifth, I was exhausted. I couldn't do any more. I said, "I think enough is enough," and I had all kinds of reasons why five was enough. Principally, I was worried about the reader, who wouldn't be able to make the transition to another couple and get interested, and so on.

I don't know how I got the idea for two chapters for each couple, but that was one of the structural ideas that I got very early on. That worked out differently in the various cases; in fact, there are three on somebody, I forget who—oh, George Eliot. There were three George Eliot chapters. So it's not as though it was sacred. In the case of the Dickens' chapters, I wrote "Dickens Dissatisfied" first, the one about his midlife crisis, then I was really up a creek because I had no material to write a second chapter. I thought, "I really am going to let my scheme down here if I only have this one chapter on Dickens. How can I do that?" It was OK to have three, but not just one. Then when I had various people read that, somebody said, "This really comes out sounding quite harsh towards Mrs. Dickens, and she seems like such a lump, and nobody will have any sympathy for her. Maybe you should put in a paragraph or even more at the start to build a picture of her as a young woman." So

I thought, "Genius! That's it. I'll do an earlier chapter. I don't have to do a later chapter—I just assumed there would be one after the other; now I can do an earlier chapter on the Dickenses when they were young, just married, and happy with each other." Then my structure really supported me there, because I think it's essential to the second chapter to have an earlier chapter.

I guess I didn't always plan to have a frame. The first part of the book that I wrote was the Carlyles' engagement chapter, the Carlyles' courtship. I really didn't know what I was going to do later. Somehow in the course of it, it occurred to me, "Ah! I have to pick them up much, much later, and of course it should go at the end of the book." Then I liked the idea of having a frame like that. It seemed appropriate. But I hadn't started out with that idea. It just grew in the course of the book. And the same thing with the prologue. The part about the Jamaica rebellion was originally part of the preface, and I can't tell you how much time it took me to write the preface to that book. I don't just mean the number of hours sitting at my desk. Months would go by, and I would be in despair about it. I would have to put it aside, unable to see any way to write it. I couldn't even reconstruct now how hard that was to write. At some point, I realized that the only way that I could get a preface that made any sense was by getting rid of that stuff about the Jamaica rebellion—it was too different. So I just consigned it to the basket and said, "OK, too bad, I really like it, but that's it." Then I had a preface that worked. That was amazing. But then I got to the end of the book, and I thought, "There really should be something more here. There still are things I haven't said about marriage that I feel like saying." So I started writing and I wrote some more, and then I thought, "Hmm, maybe I can use the material about the Jamaica rebellion here." So that was how that went.

The structure emerged in the course of writing—it was not predetermined. What was predetermined was six—then

110

five—marriages, more than one chapter on each marriage, and that was it. The rest of it was a matter of seeing possibilities in the material's development. In fact, I don't even know what the order of the last section is now, but I know that it's the reverse of what I intended. I think that I had it ending with the puppet show. That was the very end. I loved the image of Ruskin and Carlyle going off into the sunset together, these two men no longer with women, looking at a Punch and Judy show out the window. But the editor thought that that should be a preface to the conclusion in the same way that all the other little inset things were prefaces to each chapter. So I said, "OK, that just turns it around, and I don't have any strong feelings about that."

GM: By the way, the marriage that my students found most fascinating was the Dickens marriage. That's the one they wanted to discuss.

PR: That doesn't surprise me. I think that's the most fascinating to people because it's the most common situation. It's a story that almost everybody has either seen or heard. When I give lectures, it's always the one that people come up after to talk about, saying, "I know a situation just like that!" And that's exactly the kind of response I wanted. I wanted people to think about examples that they knew. What's so odd, though, is that the one that I would think just couldn't happen anymore is the Ruskins. But it turns out now I've heard over and over stories about unconsummated marriages, and the man trying to make out that the woman is crazy. I don't mean to say that there are anywhere near the same number of parallels as with the Dickenses, but I'm just surprised because I would have thought that that was completely a story of the past.

GM: You say in *Parallel Lives* that Jane Carlyle is the heroine of the book. Did you really mean that?

PR: Why do you ask?

GM: Because she's unsympathetic.

PR: Oh, really?

GM: That's my response to her.

PR: I love reading her letters. On the other hand, it's true that I don't really like her. I don't warm to her. I think she's a bit pretentious, a bit posturing, and self-important. But her spirit of resistance is the spirit I would like to pay tribute to in the book. So even if there's no personal identification or personal warmth, she's the heroine of the book in that sense. I ask why you ask the question because I can see there's something rhetorical about my saying she's the heroine.

GM: I was surprised, because George Eliot seemed to me the one you were holding out as an example. Yet when I think about the purpose for which you were writing the book, Jane Carlyle does make some sense as its exemplar.

PR: Exactly. And there are a couple of other things I can find significant when you say that, and I've never really thought about this before. It would be presumptuous to imply in any way that I identify with George Eliot. And I don't really identify with George Eliot, except in the one thing that I wrote about there, which was that—well, I can tie each of those chapters to different stages of my life; I wrote them at very different moments. When I was writing about George Eliot, my father was dying and I was just extremely sad. I never felt lonelier in my life. So I completely identified with that about her. You know, that she was so lonely and worried that she was getting older and older, never having lived, and I really think that that was my deepest identification with her, but that didn't have anything to

112

do with marriage or with what ostensibly the book was about. It seems like an accidental identification. Her age, her loneliness, and her depression in the years before she met Lewes, and my age, loneliness, and depression because my father was dying in 1980–81, when I was writing the George Eliot section.

GM: So it was with the emotions you were identifying, not with the situation?

PR: Yes. So I think of that as something beyond the pale of the book. The book isn't about that. The book is about marriage. Whatever feelings I have about George Eliot are outside of the emotional core of the book.

GM: You've indicated that writing your books has not only reflected but affected your life—for example, when you spoke of narrating Virginia Woolf's suicide. Do you find that in writing a biography, you always identify with your subject?

PR: It's not just identification. With Josephine Baker, for example, whose biography I've just finished, I would say that as long as I was writing the book, until the very end, I didn't think that I was identifying with her at all. I thought that what was going on was, I would call it "appropriation" rather than "identification." She had things that I wanted. She had psychic qualities that I wanted. When I started that book, it was very much a case of my needing things from her. How could I think I was like her? You could hardly find two people who were more different than me and Josephine Baker. So it wasn't as if I secretly felt that I was this ravishing and charming dancer. I know that those are my weak points: my body, my lack of energy, just stuff that she had that I didn't. So appropriation, I think. It's not just a question of identification.

But definitely, I use books to work out things in my own life. I don't know how you would find the energy to get through if you didn't have some sort of psychic agenda that was keeping you going. I can only tell in retrospect what it was. That is, when I'm writing a book I don't know what the thing is that I'm working out. In *Virginia Woolf*, I would say that it had to do with identity, and with work, and with achievement, with the whole notion of women's problems in achieving things. That was what I was going through at that stage of my life. I was in my late twenties, and I didn't know if it was OK for me to do anything. I mean, to have a career and to write. And all those things I thought about through Virginia Woolf, and found inspiration in her, because she was concerned with those same things, or at least I saw her as being concerned with the same things.

With *Parallel Lives,* it was—I was married from 1965 through 1975. I was married for ten years. I was divorced in 1975. And after, I started *Parallel Lives* in 1978. I wanted in retrospect to make sense out of that experience, to figure out what I thought about marriage and what it had done to my life, and whether it was necessary and so on, so that was very much a personal issue that I was working out. And I'm still not sure what it was that led me to Josephine Baker. It's still too early to say.

GM: About the biography of Josephine Baker: did you find it difficult to work on a nonliterary subject?

PR: Part of my having the nerve to do this book about Josephine Baker, who is not a literary figure, came from Justin Kaplan having decided to do a biography of Charlie Chaplin. But he abandoned that project.

GM: So you're alone now?

PR: So I'm alone. Except that Jean Strouse is writing about J. P. Morgan. The three of us who all know each other decided at more or less the same time to do nonliterary people, for I think the same kinds of reasons, the same kinds of dissatisfactions and desires to expand, and so on. But it's been very hard. It's been very hard. Imagine Jean Strouse trying to understand a kind of creativity that expresses itself in financial deals!

GM: Without written documents to work from, how did you get at those deep structures of personality we spoke of—what you call somewhere the "personal mythology," or "personal narrative" or "story"?

PR: Josephine Baker actually made her views very clear. She was somebody who worked through interviews, basically. They were her art form, her form of writing and self-expression. Everything she did was documented by reporters, and she knew how to use the press as a sounding board for herself. Of course, she really wasn't a writer, but there are a lot of people like her—for example, Mrs. Reagan, who doesn't write her memoirs, just talks them into a tape recorder then gives them to a writer to write. Josephine Baker was like that. Her personal mythology is not hard to pick up on. It comes through everything that she says. It has to do with being black. It certainly doesn't have to do with being a woman. There's no feminist ideology there at all. But her sense of who she is and what she has to prove to the world is very much based on the fact that she's black. I think that if you're looking for the central spine in somebody's life, the central organizing principle—who it is that they're proving what to—it's not that hard to find.

GM: Do you listen for images or allusions in the language? Is it anything specifically said, or just a gestalt?

PR: She talks about it quite openly. Left to her own devices, what she talks about is race. The subject is on her mind. Even when she's being a dippy chorus girl, that's what she talks about. You just have to have ears to hear. It's not in imagery. It's quite direct, what she'll say. For example, "I'm always comparing where I am now to where I was when I was in St. Louis, and I never could have lived this life had I not come to France. In America, this kind of life is impossible." It's in public statements. And it's in her actions. You know, she adopted twelve children of different races and nationalities.

GM: Is it difficult to distinguish your own perspective, your own personal mythology, from those of your subjects?

PR: Hmm. This is what I always worry about, that I'm attributing my own ideas to them.

GM: I wish you would talk a bit more about the concept, because I find it fundamental in everything you write—and also a fascinating idea.

PR: The mythology? The personal narrative? Well, I've explained it as well as I can in the preface of *Woman of Letters* and partly in the prologue to *Parallel Lives*. It's that I think you have to have some sort of conceptualization of life or life is unlivable. You have to have some narrative line, something that you see yourself as embarked upon, in order to make sense of life, in order to make decisions, in order to make sense of the past, in order to act on the future.

GM: My students felt they knew a lot about you and your personal narrative from reading *Parallel Lives*—they thought they saw it emerging from the way you told the lives.

PR: Oh, tell me what my personal mythology is!

GM: Well, they knew you were a feminist, very interested in the situation of women, someone who sees marriage and love as political rather than entirely personal, someone in conflict with society's norms.

PR: But that's my outlook, that's my mind set, but that's not my personal mythology.

GM: But isn't that an essential part of the way you structure the world, make sense of it?

PR: To me, that's something you could call my politics, or my philosophy, although I wouldn't use that word, but that's not what I mean by personal mythology or a personal narrative. And that's why I was so interested to know what they thought it was, because I don't know. And if I understand it correctly, I don't think I can know my personal mythology. If I went into analysis, perhaps I would find it out. But I've never been in analysis, and so I'm not that self-aware. If somebody else knew it, I would—

GM: So you think somebody else could tell you?

PR: I think so.

GM: Like you're revealing Josephine Baker's, or Virginia Woolf's?

PR: Yes, the organizing principles. It sounds contradictory, in the sense that you need one in order to make decisions, but it doesn't have to be conscious. You make the decisions as the result of this, but I'm enough of a Freudian to believe that sometimes the subconscious is perfectly obvious to everybody else but not to the person involved. What I'm talking about is somebody's unwritten narrative of their own life, and the weight that they give to various events in their own life—the events they choose as meaningful in the whole trajectory of their life. But maybe this isn't the right way to go about it, because it's either very obvious, or it becomes—we're pushing it so hard that it's receding.

GM: I feel like I'm turning this into a panel discussion!

PR: Oh, no, no, no, no. It's all right. I think that the best way to get at it, as I did before, is to distinguish myself from other kinds of biographers, from what I consider the normative biographer, and to say that I'm more interested in the subjective, and in the organizing principles of subjectivity, and that's what I would call a "personal mythology." I think that's a better way to get at it: describe the thing I'm interested in and then say the name that I give to it is "personal mythology." It's the subjective realm, the subjective organization that a person has for their own life. Or maybe that *I* have for their lives! That's the risk I take. The only proof that I'm right is that it's persuasive. How could you find proof that this was their own personal mythology? Especially if they couldn't know it themselves, because it's unconscious.

The burden is that it's presumptuous for somebody else to write about this, because it's really a way of saying this is what *I* think is important, this is what *I* think is organizing, these are the subjective principles that *I* believe were paramount in a person's life. But the only proof is its persuasiveness. But I don't think that the kind of things that I'm talking about, for example, the fact Virginia Woolf thought it was important that she was a woman—on the one hand, that's so completely obvious, but no one had said it before I wrote *Woman of Letters*. I mean, people just weren't talking about that kind of thing then, or writing that kind of biography.

118

Let me add that theory is not my strong point. I mean I'm not really a great theoretical thinker, and so it's a waste in a way to press me on theoretical points because you could get much better answers from another person on those points. I just don't talk well about theoretical issues. Which again is all tied up in why I write biography instead of the sort of literary criticism that's more fashionable in the academy.

GM: But your books have a strong intellectual bent to them, I think.

PR: Yes, but it's very hard to achieve. That's why the preface to *Parallel Lives* took me a year and a half, and really only the first nine pages of the preface took me that long to write because it was so much against my bent. People say in print about my books that I think so clearly, but in fact, I don't think clearly. I just am prepared to spend more time on my manuscripts than other people are on theirs to create the illusion of thinking clearly. I don't let anything go, I don't let anything be put in print until it's perfectly, perfectly clear. But it's not as though I write more easily than other people, or think more clearly. It's just that I spend more time and know where I want to get to.

In fact, I don't think that many people admire clarity and precision. I think they enjoy it, especially when they want to know what somebody has to say to them, but they tend to respect obfuscation as a sign of complexity. You see, my ideal is essentially eighteenth century: "What oft was thought but ne'er so well expressed."

GM: Are you one of those who, "with a slightly different configuration of talents"—I'm quoting you—

PR: Could have been a novelist? Yes.

GM: Are you tempted to write fiction?

PR: Yes. I think I will. I think that's what I'm going to do next.

GM: Have you been backing into it?

PR: No. No. I'm going into it absolutely foursquare. I've reached the point where I have what I consider free time. It's the one thing I've always wanted to do, and I think now it's time for me to do it if I'm ever going to do it. So I'm not backing into it, I'm going into it with my eyes open.

GM: By "backing into it," I mean this: have you been gradually letting go of what in your article "Fact and Fiction in Biography" you refer to as the support of fact that one has in writing biography? Sort of like learning to swim holding on to a float?

PR: Right. You don't have to make it all up. But also, at a certain point, what bears you up becomes something holding you back, and at that point, you shouldn't be writing biography anymore, you should be writing fiction. After this book I'm working on, I think I'll have reached that point; that I don't want to be responsible to anybody else's facts anymore. I want to make up the premises myself.

GM: So is Josephine Baker's your last biography?

PR: Well, for the moment. I don't have any other ideas. Nor do I have the desire to do another one at the moment. I can imagine coming back to Virginia Woolf and doing Virginia Woolf again. One of my models for biography is Walter Jackson Bate. He had done a little book about Samuel Johnson and then he did a big book about Samuel Johnson, and he had done a little book about Keats and then he did a big book about Keats. I've always thought that that was a possible and indeed praiseworthy thing for a biographer to do. I can see how you would put everything you know at a certain stage of your life into whatever book you write. Presumably, when I'm sixty, I'll know more than when I was thirty and can do a better job writing about Virginia Woolf.

There are other people I might do. I've gotten very interested in Willa Cather. I taught a course on Willa Cather. But I wrote a piece that's in *Writing of Women,* and that more or less took the place of writing a whole biography about her. Now, at the moment, I'm interested in Colette, but because of the language difference, I doubt that I'll end up doing a biography of Colette. Although maybe I would, I'm not sure.

GM: Does any man's life tempt you?

PR: I was tempted by Hemingway. Josephine Baker is what happened to my idea of writing about Hemingway. I started out to write about Hemingway, and I got a little grant from Wesleyan to go to Paris to do the research for Hemingway. I spent a lovely month or so in Paris one summer, but didn't get any ideas about Hemingway. But there was a poster in the Metro: "Visitez New York," with a picture of a great big black man on roller-skates listening to a ghetto blaster. And I got really interested in the fascination of the French with—it was the time that that movie *Diva* came out—I got really interested in the way the French romanticized and really loved American blacks. This book is about racial mythologies, about the way people fantasized Josephine Baker as much as it is about the way she thought about life. It's about the convergence of racial mythologies, both Europeans' in the years before the wars and hers. Her proselytizing, her desire to prove to white America what blacks could do.

GM: Do you find your publishers before you write the books, or do you write them and then look for a publisher?

PR: Now, I write a proposal to get a contract, but for the Virginia Woolf, no.

GM: So you wrote that, then looked?

PR: Exactly. And in the future, I think I would do it that way, too, because you have more freedom. If you don't need the money that you're going to get from the advance—which I did need for the Josephine Baker book. Writing the Josephine Baker book, I went on half schedule: half-time teaching. And I had gotten enough of an advance that I could afford to do that. But with fiction, I won't be able to get an advance as big as I can get for a biography. So I'm forced to going back to teaching full time. And I don't mind. In biography, both imaginatively and financially, you're borne up partly by the person you're writing about. If you choose an interesting person, the person supports you. Other people are willing to pay for a book about Josephine Baker. But if you're writing fiction, there's nobody else there to hold you up.

GM: You may be right, but people write biographies of fiction writers while nobody seems very interested in knowing about biographers themselves!

PR: You mean, readers don't feel personally about the biographers themselves? But a biographer cannot wantonly display personality. That would be a violation of the pact. As biographers go, I probably display more personality than many, but I still think it's a delicate line. You can't consider yourself more important than your subject. It's simply a violation of good taste for a biographer to think that he or she is even as important as the subject. So it becomes a very fine line. Unfortunately, the more you write, the more you get to think that you are interesting, so it becomes harder to suppress your personality.

122

I think that the interest in writers of fiction is mostly a result of people's myths about writers. What could be less interesting than a woman like Virginia Woolf who goes to bed at eleven every night, hardly ever goes out, never has any lovers, never even has sex with her husband, doesn't know how to dress? What is interesting about that life? You wouldn't want to live it. It's just the fact that people so value the artistic product that then whatever has been necessary to produce it becomes glamorous. But there's nothing glamorous about insanity, or living in the English countryside. God Almighty! I don't buy that, about the glamour of writers. I know lots and lots of writers, and essentially writing, whether it's fiction or biography, means that you're sitting in a room, by yourself, for most of the hours of the day. It's simply not glamorous. I don't know why people think it is.

Conversation with

Edwin McClellan

Although I met him in his office in the Hall of Graduate Studies at Yale, Edwin McClellan and I began our conversation at Mory's, just down the street. The maître d' and waiters knew him by name; we were seated in as quiet a corner as the tiny club afforded. I had first met this gracious man several years before, when I attended a lecture by him on modern Japanese literature. His cultivated, resonant voice brought back memories of that earlier introduction.

Woman in the Crested Kimono: The Life of Shibue Io and Her Family Drawn from Mori Ōgai's "Shibue Chūsai" is McClellan's only venture thus far into biography, but it struck me when I first read it as a unique enterprise. Interested in how other cultures perceive biography as well as in how McClellan himself might regard it, I wrote asking to meet with him. He telephoned to say that others were far better qualified to talk about biography than he, but that he would try to help if I thought he could.

After a long lunch, we walked back to his large office, which is walled with odd-sized texts, most in Japanese. There, he put me on the couch and he sat in a straight-backed chair while we finished our discussion.

Gail Mandell: One thing that intrigues me about your life of Shibue Io and her family is how hard it is to classify. In part it's translation, but it's more than that because you also interpret your source, Mori Ōgai, and change the entire emphasis of the original biography. Whatever gave you the idea of trying something so unusual?

Edwin McClellan: There were various reasons, not at all clear-cut originally. One of my main motives in writing the book was to introduce Ōgai, the biographer of Io, to the Western reader. You'll remember that I talk about him in the first few pages of the book. There have been far more exhaustive studies of Ōgai in English so that I wasn't trying in any way to do the same thing as these other studies of Ōgai have done. But I felt that somehow the real quality of Ōgai as a writer hadn't come through other studies of him. What I wanted was for the reader to understand what sort of a writer Ōgai was at his best. Some of his works of fiction and some of his historical pieces have been translated, but on the whole these translations don't do him justice. I wanted to bring Ōgai to life if I could—whether I do or not is another matter—but I wanted to show certain facets of his personality and of his literary style, and finally to convey my sense of what a great writer he was. I felt that his life of Chūsai, the doctor who was Io's husband, was perhaps his best, his most serious work. So that was one reason for my book.

The other was that I wanted to write about this particular woman. Because Ōgai was writing for a well-educated, Japanese readership, there were all kinds of things that needed explanation if what he wrote about Chūsai, the husband, or Io, the wife, was to be understood by the American or English reader. I wanted readers in this country and in England, or wherever else, to come to know a woman like her. I suppose it's almost a trite thing to say, but I think that people still have an image of Japanese women as very malleable, obedient, docile, and charming—brought up to please men; you know what I mean. This is the conventional image of Japanese women in this country, in Britain, in France, and wherever else, and it's very different from what Io herself was as portrayed by Ōgai. So I wanted to introduce a woman who lived, after all, in premodern times, who was not at all what most Westerners would imagine a representative woman of that period to have been. That was another thing I wanted to do in the book.

Another thing I wanted to do was to write about a family and in doing so to write about a particular segment of society of the time—what you might call an upper-middle-class, very well educated, enlightened family, who were on the one hand quite strict in their notion of what it was to behave but at the same time were very tolerant and terribly sophisticated, as you no doubt felt as you read about them. What I wanted was a picture of a certain way of life. I wanted to make real that way of life, which I thought most Westerners hadn't been introduced to. I wanted to show how in so many ways that society was quite different from what people might imagine upper-class or upper-middle-class life to have been in Edo, premodern Tokyo. That was another important objective that I had in mind.

You know, about the Western countries so familiar to us, a lot is known beyond the facts of institutional or economic history. But about a country like premodern Japan—Japan of that period we know as Tokugawa or Edo, which of course preceded the formal opening up of Japan—I think that very little is known about how certain people lived, even among specialists. Partly because of a certain emphasis put on the study of society by scholars in more recent times, we tend to know a lot more about how peasants lived than how such a class as Io's lived. So far as I know, very little research has been done about how a family like that—well-placed, comfortably off, educated—how such a family lived in, say, the first half or the middle of the nineteenth century.

126

Or about how such a family survived the huge upheaval of 1868. What I wanted to do was not talk so much about the economics of the survival of such a family, but the human side. I felt that nothing like that had been done before, and that it was one kind of Japanese history that needed to be written about.

GM: I was trying to think of anything at all similar to what you have done, and the only thing vaguely like it that I could come up with is Geoffrey Scott's *Portrait of Zélide,* which you may know. Both make accessible a subject treated in a much larger, rather inaccessible biography; both have the same sort of understated elegance.

EM: That's very interesting you should bring up Geoffrey Scott, because he worked with the Yale project on the Boswell papers for a while, as does my wife now. And I think he went to the same college as I, St. Andrew's in Scotland. He was a very interesting figure, Scott. Not a major figure, but extraordinarily interesting.

GM: His book wasn't a conscious influence, was it?

EM: Oh, no. No. In fact, right from the start, I was afraid that what I was doing was so far out that I hesitated to do it. Even some of the favorable reviews—and I have one in particular in mind—still start off with the question, "Exactly what is this? Where do we put it?" As though the main problem one thought of first was how would one treat such a book if one were a librarian! That was just the sort of thing I was afraid of, because that kind of question as to how to categorize or classify a work is an expression of something much deeper, which is, "What is this person doing?" You know the kind of question I mean: "Is this a literature thing, or a history thing?" People worry about that.

127

In the case of my book, some of the more sympathetic readers have tended to be sociologists or anthropologists of Japan. The person who read the manuscript for the Yale Press is an anthropologist of Japan; he was very enthusiastic about it. Amongst my colleagues, one of the most enthusiastic readers happened to be a sociologist. What I'm saying is that all this only confirmed my earlier doubts about writing such a book—in the first place writing from a text that is already written and then playing with it—making myself the narrator. Obviously, it was bound to lead to confusion in the minds of quite a lot of people, who would expect from a professor of literature something that is "literary."

GM: You mean, people would expect a critical study?

EM: Yes. Although I did try in that book to show what Ōgai was like as a writer.

GM: So it could be called criticism, biography, sociology, and history—at least. And it's translation, in part.

EM: Yes.

GM: Have you classified the book for yourself, or is that just not important to you?

EM: I couldn't really classify it. I think the Yale Press had problems with that, too. They would advertise it under "Women's Studies," then as something else—I can't remember what. Of course, East Asian Studies in general haven't been the easiest to categorize.

GM: You've talked about your scholarly reasons for wanting to write this book. You mention in your prologue that Ōgai himself may have had several personal reasons for wanting to tell Chūsai's story: one, a personal identification

128

with him because of their similar scholarly interests, and another what I took to be nostalgia for the past. Did you too have personal reasons for writing?

EM: First of all, I wouldn't call Ōgai's reason for writing "nostalgia," exactly. Not because it necessarily was not—I grant the possibility that there was nostalgia there—but I thought it was much more a sense of putting down on paper a certain way of life and a certain story of a particular time which was lost, which I think Ōgai felt only he could do. I suppose there's bound to be some nostalgia in it in the sense that he paints a very touching picture, doesn't he, of a particular way of life no longer possible in his own time. At the same time, I think he's really very careful not to sentimentalize. Too, one is always aware of Ōgai's awareness that this was only one little part of Japanese social history of the time. He had to be aware that he was not in any way touching on a much darker side of urban life in Edo. Even though he was very aware of that darker side, he chose not to write about it. His awareness would somehow make me hesitate to use the word "nostalgia." There have been many Japanese writers who have been nostalgic about the past. Was Ōgai? I think not. Then, too, he was creating a whole new literary genre. No one has written biography in Japan the way he did.

But obviously, I did have personal reasons for writing, though it's difficult to say what they were. I admired Ōgai tremendously, and felt that it was high time somebody showed what depth and humanity there was to this man. He's normally seen as a terribly severe, austere, half-military figure: he was in the army, in the medical corps. I wanted to bring his personal qualities out. That was as personal as anything, because I really cared about this man's reputation among Western readers and among Western specialists, who all seemed to have a one-sided view of him. I wanted to make the prevailing view of him more complex than it was.

Also, I shared with Ōgai his great attachment to Io. We see in Ōgai's book how he becomes increasingly attached to her. Although he's hardly ever personal in the book, there are some wonderfully resounding passages where he reveals his admiration for her.

The other thing I wanted to do was to introduce Io as a remarkable person. I felt very strongly that Western readers should know that in the first half of the nineteenth century such a woman could in fact exist and survive as well as she did—as a widow. It's a remarkable story. I found her attractive—there's no question about it. I had a great deal of personal feeling about her—that is, I felt attracted to Io as a woman, whether or not she is a product of Ōgai's imagination and art. *Not,* I think. It's far more likely that she really did live more or less the way Ōgai says and was historically more or less the way Ōgai creates her, and that authenticity adds much to her attractiveness to me. That makes her unusually attractive in a way that no character of fiction can quite be.

GM: You mean, because she had an independent existence?

EM: Yes. And ironically, perhaps such a woman portrayed in a work of fiction of that time might seem too unlikely and wouldn't be believed. You do have valorous women, in fact martial women, being depicted in the fiction, but they just don't have the depth that Io has.

Although Ōgai never really criticizes her, he doesn't close his eyes to Io's failings as a person. We know what that wonderful daughter of hers—Kuga, the one who becomes a singer; a wonderful portrait in itself, I think; small but wonderful—we know that Kuga suffers because of Io. When Io has lost her favorite daughter and Kuga says to her, "I bet you wish it had been me," Io—and Ōgai—make no comment. It's very moving, because you know that somehow or another, Kuga has perceived the truth that her mother favored the other child in an almost unbelievable way. You see that Ōgai sees Io's favoritism quite clearly, yet he doesn't explain it, doesn't excuse it, doesn't exploit it, just allows it to stand—beyond comment, but a fact. This is a willful woman; she's no saint.

GM: Do you think of her as an exception to most women of her time? Or might there have been many Ios in families of her day and class?

EM: I suspect so. I don't say there were an overwhelming number of Ios; of course not. Far more standard is her sister, for example, the one who runs away from her husband. Later, Io has that argument with him—do you remember?

GM: Yes, and when he dies Io takes care of her sister and her daughter—builds them a little house, in fact—because the woman's incapable of surviving without someone to protect her. That's an effective contrast between the two sisters.

EM: The sister may have been more typical. Nevertheless, Io can't have been all that much of an exception. That is, most men accept her as an admirable woman. There are also obvious hints that some are very attracted to her, like her foster brother. Remember the wonderful letter he wrote her about widowhood—describing what it was like to be a widow, offering her protection because no one ever paid any attention to widows? How wonderfully true and sensitive that man's perception was—we know it to be true now—I mean, far truer than we like to think. You can read between the lines that this man, obviously very decent, had more than a brotherly affection for her. So she can't have been that much of an exception.

131

GM: I suppose you could argue that in Japanese society he was a "macho" man, likely to reject a woman who seemed too much of an exception to the norm.

EM: Yes, very macho—a warrior, in fact—a genuine example of the "bushi." Like warriors everywhere, he was one who loved his horse above everything. How universal that is! You could just as well be speaking about an English cavalry officer.

But to return to Io, I don't think she would have been singular, by any means—rather, she was distinguished, impressive, as was her daughter Kuga.

GM: As you say, Kuga's another wonderful character. You almost want her story to go on.

EM: In fact, Ōgai spends quite a lot of time on Kuga—on her professional life, in particular. But I don't go into that, because I thought it would break the symmetry of the book. In all honesty, however, I must tell you that Ōgai does give her quite a bit of space. Because he is attracted to her also.

GM: Did you leave out other things from Ōgai's book? In particular, did you cut out much of Chūsai's life in order to stress Io's story?

EM: I would guess that Chūsai's life takes up about half of Ōgai's book. Proportionally, that's about the same as in mine. But there's constant reference back to Chūsai in Ōgai's book. While Ōgai is writing about Io he starts each chapter with the statement that such and such a year was so and so year after Chūsai died, so as to constantly remind us of the presence of Chūsai. Ōgai makes it clear that he tells Io's story out of reverence for Chūsai, to honor him. He feels he owes it to such a man to tell the story of those he left behind.

GM: Is that perhaps because of a tendency in Japanese culture to identify a person by his family, so that telling the story of one's family would seem more appropriate in a Japanese life?

EM: Yes. There, the whole notion of name is terribly important; I mean the surname itself is very important, and any person, adopted or no, who carries that name in his own generation is as much a representative of that name as he is an individual. I think there's a great sense of that in Ōgai—he's very concerned about who Chūsai's ancestors were, although that doesn't come through so much in my book. If I had gone into it in the excessive way that Ōgai goes into it, it would have put the reader to sleep!

GM: Your book makes it seem that Ōgai was as much telling Io's story as Chūsai's. Is that your own emphasis, or is that the impression Ōgai's book leaves you with?

EM: Well, I have perhaps come to think that I exaggerate the importance of Io at the expense of Chūsai, although I didn't do that consciously—I didn't intend to exaggerate Io's importance. And I do think Io is terribly important—in fact, most Japanese readers would say that if it hadn't been for Io, they would have found the book formidable, austere, and perhaps boring. That is pretty well agreed, I think. In that sense, I don't think it's inexact to say that Io is a crucial figure in Ōgai's book. How Ōgai really felt about this, I can't say. I think that he may not have wished to see Chūsai displaced, because he may have found Chūsai's life somehow terribly interesting, terribly important to himself, because of the way he identified with him, and even though Chūsai doesn't come through as a terribly interesting person, and Io does, Ōgai himself would have wanted to preserve Chūsai's dignity. On the other hand, there's no doubt about it that Ōgai is at his most lively when he writes about Io. But would he have said that Io was a more important person than Chūsai? No, I don't think that at all.

I suppose another question that I have asked myself is how much I was moved to emphasize Io by the increasing interest in women. I suppose that I couldn't have helped but be influenced by my own growing awareness of women's issues.

GM: But it wasn't in the front of your mind?

EM: I don't think it was, though it might have seemed so to some people. I've always been interested in Io, and my interest in her didn't result from my own increased awareness of women's issues, because my education there started happening rather late. But I must have felt—yes, of course!—I did feel that the fact that someone like Io did exist, did manage to survive, did manage to maintain her dignity and originality—in relative terms, mind you—was important to communicate. I thought that her example in itself could be terribly important.

GM: You also added to Ōgai's work, didn't you?

EM: In the notes, for example. People don't normally look at the notes. I don't intend that they spend time on them; I don't want the enjoyment that they have reading the book spoiled by constant reference to notes. But what I tried to do in the notes and in the book itself took a lot of research. Here, Richard Torrance, a graduate student at Yale, was enormously helpful. There really was a lot of research work involved in determining, for example, sociological factors—the class of the family, where their income came from, what it meant to Io to be an exile, in what sort of social circumstances she would find herself. So there's a great deal of that sort of information in the book and in the notes.

134

GM: Much of the information about Io, and Chūsai for that matter, came down through their son, Tamotsu, isn't that right? Did he write it down, or did Ōgai interview him?

EM: Essentially, he wrote it all down. For the most part, his notebooks are still available in Tokyo. The notes that I used, in fact, were actually Tamotsu's notes, which had been printed thanks to a scholar of Ōgai, who collected and reprinted all the notes that Tamotsu wrote for Ōgai's benefit. I depended very heavily on those accounts.

But with these accounts, one has to depend not only upon one's own sense of what sounds authentic and what doesn't but also upon Ōgai's sense of what sounded authentic. Very difficult! There is no question about it, though: Ōgai trusted Tamotsu. He had a great respect for Tamotsu's integrity, even if he might occasionally discount something because he felt that when it was told to Tamotsu it was distorted somehow—inexact or embellished—perhaps by Io herself. Because Io told a lot of these stories to her son.

I don't think that Ōgai himself could have said much more about Io, because more information was not available to him. On the other hand, it is also true that the relative thinness of his material helped bring out his very best qualities as a writer—his dignity and reserve. I suspect that he saw all he wanted to see, that he felt that he'd got to know all he needed to know about Io. To start explaining or understanding people of her generation in sophisticated modern terms, Ōgai would have thought presumptuous. It was not important for him to know whether in fact she wept bitterly when Chūsai died. As you know, there's no mention of her reaction to his death. So I wonder how much more Ōgai would have told us, even if he had more information. In a way, for Ōgai to write about people of the past required precisely the sort of limitations that he suffered from. I guess it's that kind of reticence in Ōgai, that refusal finally to pry—perverse enough in a biographer, I suppose—that makes Ōgai admirable in my eyes. Of course, his approach is very different from that of contemporary Western biographers who try to reveal the inner lives of their subjects.

GM: Do you agree that there's a difference in the way he tells Chūsai's story and Io's story? It strikes me that Chūsai's story is more conventionally told in that it focuses on his achievements and characteristics. On the other hand, Io—and especially her actions—is more precisely observed. But perhaps that's because Tamotsu did not know his father but recalled his mother vividly.

EM: Precisely. And I also suspect that Ōgai found her a much more interesting person.

GM: Ōgai was a novelist also, wasn't he, even though you say he didn't feel comfortable writing fiction. Maybe she appealed to the novelist in him.

EM: Yes, he wrote some wonderful fiction, but I don't think he wanted to go on with it. You see, when you're writing realistic fiction, you have certain obligations as a writer—you have to go into detail, provide more analysis and give a fairly complex portrait of a person. I think he tired of that necessity and wanted to create a different kind of literature.

He really doesn't give us what you could call an in-depth portrait of anybody. I think his biography of Chūsai is an expression of a certain desire on Ōgai's part to get into a world where the modern sort of perception was made irrelevant, didn't have much to do with what really was important about the person; one that offered another way of looking at human character and behavior. I think that what he was trying to do in that book was to say, "Look, I'm trying to create a way of life in which people were judged differently." I think he's trying to paint a way of life which although on the one hand was extremely cultured and sophisticated, on the other hand was far more straightforward and far less fraught with complications than life today.

GM: It sounds as though you may have wanted that too, in choosing to make Ōgai accessible to us.

EM: I wanted to try to express my understanding of Ōgai's need to write about such a way of life. I thought that this was a very profound perception on his part, and yes, I suppose that I have to say I kind of share that. It becomes so personal and perhaps almost pretentious to say, but I am moved by what I would call Ōgai's reverence, or piety. I am moved by it, and I suppose that insofar as I am capable of being moved by it, I share some of it.

I think that maybe my book is annoying to many people because of my ready acceptance of Ōgai's reverence, of what some people might perceive to be a very superstitious, conservative side to Ōgai. A lot of modern academic people might see Ōgai's notion of what is important about a past way of life as an impossibly limited, self-indulgent, perhaps even elitist way of looking at the past. And not only that, but superstitious in the sense that Ōgai expresses such thoughts as that in honoring a man long dead we owe it to that person to write about those he left behind. To write in such language as that is not what you would call highly rational. It's simply an expression of faith, of piety, right? Something rather religious in its way. And my uncritical acceptance of Ōgai's statement would also be seen as a mark of something perversely superstitious or irrational. Don't you think so? I suppose my own book is a book in which I try to express that side of myself, too.

GM: Was his life of Chūsai the only biography Ōgai wrote?

EM: No, he wrote others. This one of Chūsai was his first major biography, but for some years before he wrote that, he was very interested in history and wrote various accounts of past events. From there, writing about particular people involving particular events wasn't much of a jump. This was his first, really sustained major work in the genre. It was both biographical and historical.

GM: Did Ōgai know Western biography?

EM: Yes, he must have known. As I point out in the prologue, he studied in Germany. How much of English biography he knew I don't know—probably very little.

GM: You say he had no Japanese models to follow.

EM: Not really.

GM: He was then creating his own form?

EM: Very much so.

GM: Would you say that Ōgai is the major Japanese biographer—if indeed one can speak of a biographical tradition in Japan?

EM: Biography, strangely enough, is not a highly developed genre in Japan. There isn't even a word in Japanese that quite corresponds to the word "biography" in English, although I guess that the word that is used for his biographies in Japanese is close enough. And I suppose that if you were to use that particular word, which is *shiden,* you would automatically think of Ōgai. Since his time—he died in 1922 at the age of sixty—other famous studies of people of the past have been written. But I would say that by virtue of the fact that Ōgai is one of the great literary figures of modern times in Japan—there's only one other writer of his time who compares with him in stature—by virtue of that fact alone, whatever he wrote is bound to attract the kind of attention that works of other writers wouldn't, whatever their character might be.

GM: Are more biographies being written now, owing to whatever reasons—influence from the West, for example?

EM: I don't get that impression. Ever since I was a boy, I myself have always been fond of biography. I enjoyed reading biographies and also travel books—serious travel books. And I have continued reading certain biographies. Our children, for example, knowing this, constantly pick up biographies for me. Both of them used to live in England until very recently. Now only our daughter lives there; our son is in this country. Very recently, the two of them bought me a life of Charles Laughton, a wonderful book about Laughton the actor and person as well as a wonderful book on acting. And I was thinking, "Would such a book have been written in Japan?" And the answer is, "No, I don't think so."

GM: Can you say why not?

EM: I should be able to say why not, but I'm not sure I can. But I was going to ask, is a book like that as popular in this country as it is in England? I just don't know whether American readers have the same interest—I don't necessarily mean the same degree of interest—but the same kind of interest in certain types of biography as English readers seem to. I'm not so sure. It's an interesting question.

One answer to your question might be that the English have inherited, from when, I don't know, a great interest in manners, in particular sorts of societies, such as the society of actors, and the hierarchies within it. For example, when you read about someone like Evelyn Waugh—his is another life I read recently—you know that a book like that wouldn't have been written in Japan, partly because the sort of social concerns that someone like Evelyn Waugh had, and also suffered from, would seem outlandish in Japan. Maybe some of those things that make a biography interesting to the Westerner are some of those very things that make English society sometimes so offensively snobbish. What partly makes the life of Evelyn Waugh so interesting is the fascination the reader feels about this life of a man who made an art of snobbery, who was obsessed with nuances of place, schooling and all of that. But these concerns don't exist in Japan in quite the same way. Not to say that Japan is a democratic country in a way that Britain isn't, but I think that it doesn't have the ingredients—politically, socially, or whatever—that would make for the same kind of biography or autobiography that can be written in Britain.

GM: It seems that even apart from content, this kind of literature is one that hasn't caught on in Japan, for whatever reasons—perhaps, as you suggest, different social realities, different values, different interests.

EM: I agree. Maybe also the English have a certain insatiable curiosity about aspects of another person's life or about one's psyche. I'm not so well informed about this, but I would suspect that gossip as an art, say, has reached heights in England it perhaps could never reach in Japan.

GM: I suppose curiosity about others' lives often does reduce to gossip—to a desire to know and tell secrets.

EM: I don't mean this in a mischievous sense, but I wonder whether gossip isn't more of a practiced art in England than it is in the States. That also may have something to do with one's notion of what biography should be or can be.

GM: Given that curiosity, it seems to me that, at least from the West's point of view, biography offers a good way of bridging the gap between East and West.

EM: Yes, I agree with you.

GM: For example, looking at the life of Io and her family, one feels very close to an alien way of life. Was bridging cultures one of your purposes in retelling Io's story?

EM: Oh, very much so. Absolutely right. No matter how well acquainted the American reader is with, say, Japanese literature, I suspect that the perception of what Japan is really like is never the same when based on fiction as when revealed through what is, ostensibly at least, mostly true. At least, that's the way I feel. Before finishing the book, I gave lectures on Io at various places, and I felt that for all the most simple, human reasons, people responded to the reality of Io in a way that they couldn't have to a figure of fiction. No matter how lacking in depth the portrait of Io may be or how naive some of the anecdotes about her may be, nevertheless, the mere fact that these are stories told about a person who really lived carries a certain weight and conveys a validity that no story about a figure of fiction can. Do I make sense?

GM: I think so. It seems to me that one of the great attractions of biography is that no matter how much interpretation may enter into the telling of a life, the reader still has a deep sense of entering into another existence, one that occurred outside the imagination.

EM: Also, I think there are certain happenings in any life which are in themselves quite simple and ordinary, but we ourselves bring meaning to them, partly because of their simplicity. Like Io's relationship to her stepson. That's a wonderful relationship. The love there is very convincing, very moving. Perhaps nothing in fiction can carry the kind of persuasiveness that biography can when told so simply, so almost naively as Ōgai tells it.

Then, too, as in no other kind of literature, one has the sense of the meaning of history to individuals. For example, through the account of Tamotsu's attempt to entertain his impoverished foster uncle and his family when he had no money himself, one sees the kinds of changes that had taken place in their society. It's only through books such as this that one gets the idea of what it meant in such a very foreign culture for a person to have experienced a revolution and to find himself or herself in a totally changed social circumstance. It's very difficult for us to feel the reality of things like that otherwise, don't you think?

But to return to the question of bridging the gaps between cultures, I think it's a very difficult thing to do. I suppose I don't have that much faith in the capacity of peoples of very different cultures to transcend certain barriers. On the other hand, I'm not that pessimistic, either. What I was trying to do in this book was to reach the sort of reader who would understand the sort of belletristic endeavor that I was engaged in. I wanted the reader to understand that I was writing essentially as—what?—an essayist, I suppose. I wanted a reader who would be sensitive to my use of language, to the nuances of my diction, who then, through that, would understand certain traits in another culture. I felt that to recognize the essential, human traits of the people in Io's world would first require of the reader a sensitivity to the English language. Of course, that demand may have presented yet another obstacle to understanding! It's not often that you can be sure of readers who are sensitive to the way you use your language, especially if you're using a kind of language that has barely survived in the English literary tradition. I'm afraid there are not that many people today, certainly among academics, who write in that vein.

When I wrote the book, I did so with a certain conscious sense of a particular literary heritage. I guess this sounds presumptuous, but when you mentioned Scott, I was fascinated, because it's precisely that sort of writer whom I admired and read a lot of when I was young. Such writers could have been academics, and perhaps sometimes were, but often were not. They were people who were in an interesting twilight world, I suppose you might say.

Anyway, I think that it can be as difficult for a writer like that to get through to some of my fellow Japanese specialists, as it is to get through to the lay reading public. The literate lay reader would perhaps be—no, quite obviously would be—more sensitive to my language than many of my colleagues in the field of Japanese literature.

GM: This problem of audience seems to connect with what we were talking about earlier—the problem of classifying a book like yours. Chances are you might have found more of the readers you desire in an earlier century—those I suppose you could call "cultivated" people.

EM: Possibly. I do think, as I said earlier, that some of the most sensitive readers of my book were not Japanese scholars at all, but those who seemed to understand the language I was using and who therefore had an innate sensitivity to what a culture like Io's was like.

GM: I'm intrigued with point of view in the book. That's one of the ways in which the book was most interesting to me. In telling any life, you have numerous points of view, but in this case there are several narrators: Tamotsu, probably retelling what Io herself had told him, Ōgai retelling that, and then you yourself with a further narration.

EM: I found that terribly difficult to do without seeming incongruous or terribly inconsistent. So I had to be very,

143

very careful not to allow my voice to become too obtrusive—to allow Ōgai to speak, but at the very same time to have my own interpretation subtly color the reader's understanding of what Ōgai was saying.

GM: So in a sense you become the intermediary between his culture and ours, his age and ours?

EM: I think so. I was very conscious of doing that.

GM: Did you feel you could do justice to—remain faithful to—both traditions, both of which in fact you share?

EM: I don't know. Obviously, if my mother hadn't been Japanese, I might not have had the same sense of attachment to Io. By attachment, I mean I might not have had that sense almost of obligation to introduce a person like Io to the Western reader. That part of my heritage I'm sure played a part in my desire to bring to life a woman like Io. That is, indeed, the fact that my mother was Japanese, although I never really knew her. She died when I was an infant. But I suppose that gave me a sense of identification with Io. Don't you find that likely, or possible?

On the other hand, I suspect that the kind of book that this is has at the same time something to do with my other half, which is English. That is, as a literary effort it has the English belletristic quality I was speaking of—especially in its light style, if you like. I was interested in writing a work that would sit easily, one that was perhaps more implicit than certain other kinds of writing.

GM: Were the influences on your style all English or did you grow up reading Japanese as well?

EM: Not really. I grew up sort of bilingual. That is, I spoke both languages, although a person is never truly bilingual. One language always takes over. But insofar as anyone is bilingual, I suppose I was. But not when it came to reading and writing. My formal education was entirely in English. Although it helped for me to speak Japanese, the literary side of the language was initially self-taught and then more formally learned later.

GM: Would you like to write another biography?

EM: What I'm tempted to do right now is actually something a bit different. There's a very famous Japanese novelist who died some years ago, an immensely popular writer of historical romances—historical novels, really. He was essentially and I think quite unashamedly a popular writer and wrote an enormous amount, all historical and set in premodern times, and all extremely successful. I just don't know what my assessment of him today would be if I were to reread some of his novels, but what I recently read by him that moved me very, very much was a collection of childhood memories of growing up in Yokohama in the most appalling poverty. His father, who was once moderately successful as a businessman, failed very badly and—always inclined to drink—became very much a drunkard. His wife—this writer's mother—kept the family together, and it's a story of how this family survived.

My own feeling is that this book is a more impressive piece of literature than many of the novels he wrote. It's about growing up in Yokohama, which really is a very interesting city. It came into existence after the opening up of Japan and was a very different city from cities like Tokyo and Kyoto, which were great cities before the arrival of Perry. So it gives you a picture of life in the late nineteenth century in this interesting city—a picture of what it was like to be genteel but shockingly poor. And also a picture of family relationships in terrible circumstances.

What I want to do is translate this book, and at the same

145

time, once again, build up a picture of what I think has to be built up for the Western reader, that is, I would fill in certain gaps which the Japanese reader would not be troubled by. And also perhaps introduce a sociological/historical context to explain not only the city itself but the time and also things about a family like this which the writer doesn't think to make clear.

What I would like it to be is a sort of translation-commentary with interpretative notes which would give the Western reader the sense of the reality of at least one family living in the late nineteenth century—of what poverty meant to them, especially to the mother, who managed to keep this family together despite mistreatment of her, and their near-starvation diet. The book itself is almost this man's homage to his mother—very moving.

GM: It sounds as if it has some of the same ingredients as Io's story, particularly in the recreation of a historical period through a life.

EM: Yes, it does. I suppose I've always loved fiction, but I also love history and biography as much. In fact, my training as an undergraduate was in history, not in literature. And I still continue to take great delight in history.

Conversation with

Jonathan Spence

Over the phone, Jonathan Spence gave me directions to the Naples Pizzeria, where he suggested we meet for breakfast. The tall man who introduced himself to me had a bushy beard and wore a Ragg wool pullover and wash pants. His manner was disarmingly candid. We got our mugs of coffee and English muffins at a counter, then sat in one of the booths carved with graffiti. I piled my copies of Spence's books, which I had brought with me, to one side of the table. At this time of the morning, the place was quiet except for an occasional clanging tray.

For years Spence's books have delighted me. I first read *The Death of Woman Wang* (1978) because of my passion for Asian literature. That slim book destroyed any preconceived notions I might have had about genre. In it, Spence tells the story of a peasant woman who ran away from her husband, and the consequences of that act, no doubt the most significant decision of her life. By weaving together historical records, literary sources, and the notebooks of a public official, the author recreates the context in which these events occurred—the disaster-plagued, seventeenth-century town of T'an-ch'eng in China's Shantung province.

Finally, Spence takes his reader into a place more strange even than T'an-ch'eng—the mind of Woman Wang herself. Most surely, this was literature, history, and biography of a radically different sort, I decided.

Backtracking, I next read an earlier book, *The Emperor of China: Self-Portrait of K'ang-hsi* (1974), in which Spence uses the seventeenth-century Emperor K'ang-hsi's autobiographical writings to create a portrait of the man. Through a montage of personal reflections, letters, and public statements, the man behind the public figure emerges. This, I quickly followed with *The Memory Palace of Matteo Ricci* (1984), a study of a sixteenth-century Jesuit missionary to China constructed around a text he wrote to demonstrate his technique of memorization. Spence uses Ricci's mnemonic devices as a way of entering Ricci's experience and, ultimately, his mind.

In a book published since our conversation, *The Question of Hu* (1988), Spence continues his unorthodox explorations of the human mind and experience in his narration of the journey of an eighteenth-century Chinese gatekeeper to France. He describes this last work near the end of our interview.

Gail Mandell: Your books *The Emperor of China, The Death of Woman Wang,* and *The Memory Palace of Matteo Ricci* are the ones I'd like to concentrate on. These are some of the most unconventional biographies I've read. Many biographers seem to be straining against the chronological form as too confining. And you seem to solve that dilemma.

Jonathan Spence: Yes, sometimes.

GM: I wonder if you think of your books as biographies and yourself as a biographer?

JS: It took me a long time to get used to being called that, because I suppose I thought of myself as a historian who was experimenting with the form in which historical work was usually presented, which I sometimes found less than fascinating. I've never understood why research has to be so separated from the public domain. It doesn't make any sense to me.

In fact, I have usually read much more about the background than about the person I've allegedly studied. Yet I began to realize that I was always writing about people and concentrating on the environment around one person. Then people began saying I was a biographer. But to me a biographer did these immense two-volume studies of famous writers like Tolstoy or huge studies of Napoleon. You know, I hadn't really thought of myself as this sort of biographer, and I still don't. I think I just pursue an idea that happens to be based on an individual life. I'm still not used to the term, really.

GM: Your work is so interdisciplinary—it's hard to call it one thing or another. I didn't know what your field was when I first read your books.

JS: Well, that's because I wasn't trained in university in Chinese studies at all. I was educated in general world history and then only switched to Chinese when I came to the States and when I had already finished my undergraduate degree.

GM: Was that the influence of a teacher?

JS: The switching was partly the influence of Mary Wright, who helped very much—yes, kept me in the field. But it was otherwise just a generalized interest in China, which I'd never had a chance to follow up in undergraduate school because in England there was very little Chinese.

There was only one course at my university, I think, which I never took. And so I made the jump, for fun, but behind that lies a deeper interest in European cultures.

GM: May I ask you, what is your idea of biography? And how do you see it relating to history and literature, and perhaps psychology?

JS: I was thinking about this driving in and feeling that probably the biographer is actually looking for something he lacks or can't find. I think it's a more precise quest than other kinds of historical writing. I think you're trying to enter somebody else's mind. At least, that's my definition of biography. I know how hard that is; I know how hard it is to know even one's own mind, let alone somebody else's! I'm not sure whether the subject of the biographer is a victim or not. I've thought a lot about that. You know, the person can't fight back. In a sense it's up to your integrity to make that quest as deep as you can. And sometimes you have almost nothing to go on. *Woman Wang* is only ten lines to go on. But for some reason that text fascinated me.

I think that biography is a search. Ultimately it's a search for self-understanding. Some people can find this by studying normal historical trends. For me it's zeroing in on the single life that gives me—not satisfaction; well, let's just say that's what I focus on.

GM: It seems to me that these three works in particular do somehow convincingly manage to get inside the minds of the subjects, just as you were saying you tried to do.

JS: Good.

GM: Does that then explain your inventive forms? Is it an attempt to do that sort of probing that leads you to the creative forms you use?

JS: Right. The form has never existed before the book in my case, in every one of these three books. Indeed, in everything—the book I'm doing now—the form grew slowly out of the material as I tried to draw the ideas forth. It's not that I'm opposed to chronological biography—at all—I read it with pleasure. It's just that I think that the organizing principles behind our own lives and our own memories are not chronological. It's a layman's psychology, I guess, a layman's Freudian insight. From what little I know about books on memory, I would say that because we emphasize certain things regardless of when they happened in our lives, we distort the chronology around them. We lose track of certain things, perhaps in middle age, and go back to things in childhood. Five years are dominated by a one-minute conversation. I think in a way we all know that. My quest is to try to find such moments. For example, with *K'ang-hsi,* at the very end of the book I got the idea of using that valedictory to illuminate such moments.

GM: That came at the end?

JS: Yes.

GM: I would have guessed that you started with that document and designed the book to illuminate it.

JS: No. The book originally began with the letters to the eunuchs, which ended up as an appendix. The whole point of the book almost disappeared. I mean the original trigger almost vanished. Because it was originally a quest for the authentic voice of K'ang-hsi out hunting. I was going to use those documents and then branch out perhaps into more chronological thought. But that vanished somewhere along the line.

GM: But the letters do end up last, which is in a sense first when you've finished.

JS: Yes, because that's the one that's left in your mind. The *Woman Wang* changed again and again and again. It was only long after I had finished that I realized that what I was saying in that book was that her death was the earthquake. Starting with the earthquake wasn't a conscious decision, it just felt right to begin there, and then somehow equate the shakiness of the community with a literal shaking. Actually, I was beginning to write that just after the huge T'ang-shan earthquake in China, in which certainly hundreds of thousands of people died—actually quite near where Woman Wang lived.

The *Ricci* was again very slow in developing its form. Each of the books is based around one single text, of course, which is the way I like to write. The *Ricci* was the memory text, and I very slowly got the idea of using the images themselves to organize it instead of its chronology, making the jump which some reviewers haven't liked. But many others did, so there's a complete split among the reviewers. Some of them asked how the hell did I know that the memory images would have been significant to him? And the only answer is that in my gut, I know. I don't think he would have chosen memory images that didn't matter to him. But I can't prove it. I just chose to use them as organizing principles.

GM: I see in this book and in the others a movement that is perhaps best described in the last passage of *Matteo Ricci*—let's see if I can find it:

"It often happens," he writes, "that those who live at a later time are unable to grasp the point at which the great undertakings or actions of this world had their origin. And I, constantly seeking the reason for this phenomenon, could find no other answer than this, namely that all things (including those that come at last to triumph mightily) are at their beginnings so small and faint in outline that one cannot easily convince oneself that from them will grow matters of great moment."

JS: Yes, I love that passage. Those are his own words. All three passages that make up the end of that book, which to me is the best thing I've ever written, were all things that I couldn't use in the book. I loved them so much, but I couldn't find where to put them. When I'd finished the draft and was not sure where I was going, I found these—I mean I still had these. The wonderful thing was that they summarized his entire life's work. And the passage from his letters also remained, the one about his already taking on the attributes of old men, thinking always of time past, which is such a strange anticipation of Proust in its way. Realizing that I hadn't even used them was just eerie until suddenly they all came together in a complete chapter.

GM: I feel that about the book—that everything comes together at the end. That's true of all your books and is the movement I was describing: from the many and faint to the particular and mighty. There are so many disparate elements, especially in a book like *Woman Wang*.

JS: Yes, yes.

GM: And it's hard to see how all of these elements are coming together until the final chapter. The last sequence of *Woman Wang,* which takes the reader into her mind, is a good example.

JS: Right. Some people think that's very naughty, and they may be right.

GM: It may be more accepted as a technique in fiction than in history.

JS: Yes. I mean, I like the book to change as you're reading it—the way our memories do and our emotions do.

GM: It constantly needs reinterpretation.

JS: So at the very end, the reader says, "Oh, so that's what I've been reading!"

GM: It's a revelation—

JS: "So that's what it is!"

GM: —an experience, or an insight. And I think you're providing the context for awareness.

Now for some specific questions about the books. You say of Woman Wang that she took you into T'an-ch'eng. What was so remarkable about her and her story that you decided to subordinate everything else to it—those wonderful stories of P'u Sung-ling, for example, or the chronicles?

JS: She was the trigger for the whole book. It wouldn't have existed without her, so in a sense I found all the other things after. As I said, I came across that case totally by chance. Once I'd found it, I decided to try to give it the richest context possible. But I knew that was all there was on the case, so I could either have a ten-line book or I could elaborate. So I just tried to think of everything that might somehow illuminate that one moment. Now, why I went after that one moment is very difficult to answer. I don't know. The book was meant to be as total a reversal as possible of the *Emperor of China* book. Having in a sense thought about absolute power in the Emperor book, I tried to think about absolute powerlessness. For a long time, I was thinking of something on the peasant man—you know, peasant life in China—to counterpoise the imperial. But then I guess when I found this case, I suddenly made the

154

leap, saying, "Of course, it would be a peasant *woman* who would embody this side of Chinese society." That made the whole point about this side of Chinese society. So once I got that idea, I decided to stick with it.

GM: Did you then set out to write a study of woman's situation in China? That's very strong in the book, I think.

JS: In a way. But no, I was really just trying to give the context of her death. I was pretty sure that would be a study of women in China. I mean, because I think she died as a woman, not as a person, not as an inhabitant of Shantung.

GM: Because she was a woman, she died?

JS: Yes, I think she died the way she died *because* she was a woman. And I found that very sad.

GM: Of course, the women in the stories are so powerful, by contrast.

JS: Several people have pointed this out to me; they've said the other women in the stories have terrific intelligence and resourcefulness. And I've said, "But those are fiction."

GM: That's something Virginia Woolf points out: the strange paradox between woman's role in history and her role in literature. In the latter, she's so powerful but in the former so impotent.

JS: That was not conscious, again, when I was writing. Quite a few people use this book in seminars. I was talking to one woman scholar recently who said they had just had the most wonderful seminar entirely on this idea of the powerlessness versus the power of the women in the book. She said to her amazement half the students, who knew no

155

Chinese, could remember the names of all the different women.

GM: Another aspect of the book that fascinated me was the different ways of coping with disaster. One is the story-telling form by which P'u Sung-ling is able to cope with such harsh realities.

JS: I think he is. It helps him confront the disasters of his own life, I suppose, by writing about the disasters of others in that way.

GM: And his readers? I would think it would help them transcend them, too.

JS: That's hard to know, because he wrote very difficult Chinese, and it's hard to know how widely these circulated, whether it was just in a small, elite group. It would have been too hard to have been read by most people, I think. There is a lot of work now slowly beginning to be done on P'u Sung-ling as people decide that he's a really major figure in Chinese literature. So I think that in the next decade or so we're going to see massive studies. I know of several that are going on now.

GM: I think the last part of the book is extremely beautiful, where you weave a fabric of Woman Wang's possible fantasies and associations at the moment of her death, using much of P'u's imagery.

JS: Did it depress you?

GM: No, not at all. The beauty of the piece redeemed everything for me.

JS: I'm so glad.

GM: But some of my students find it depressing.

JS: They haven't lived long enough.

GM: Have you had much criticism from other historians, personalizing history as you do?

JS: Some. From some people. But not enough to depress me unduly. Some aren't sure I should be doing what I'm doing. But I think there's room for lots of different kinds of writing. I don't want any kind of a school. I get occasional letters saying, "Tell me how to do it like you." And I have said, "No, do it your way." I'm not going to run a course on *Woman Wang* and *Emperor of China.* That's just the way those particular books happened to come out. I'm not preaching any particular genre.

GM: Or trying to revolutionize historical writing?

JS: No.

GM: About *The Emperor of China,* you call it a montage and have said that you found its inspiration in Marguerite Yourcenar's *Memoirs of Hadrian.* How did you determine what to put where? Did you leave out very much of what he had written?

JS: Yes. There's a huge amount. It's the opposite of the *Woman Wang* problem. There are millions of words on K'ang-hsi. But I figured the ones that were really personal were not that numerous. Essentially, the very, very first version of that book had been a public discourse using the approach of the seven ages of man. The first essay I ever did, the first little talk I gave on K'ang-hsi was literally based on the seven ages. This man lets us unravel the emperor more than usual, because he really does talk about being a little child, and he does talk about being old and querulous—in the last of the "Shakespearean stages." So I suggested we really could do a "Seven Ages of K'ang-hsi," and that got me thinking. That little paper was very well received. In fact, it was quite a major moment in my career; people got very excited—now, sometimes at a conference they do—and saw it as very original. As they were getting more and more excited, I was getting less and less so. Then I began to think, "Well, let's hold off for a little and not involve Shakespeare. Let's try to think of what the major rhythms in this active, powerful person's psyche would have been. And I decided this idea of youthful restlessness and violence, what I called "In Motion," was the first. And then I built on the difference between trying to put ideas into practice and what I just called thinking. Then the whole mixture of family and the sexual side, which one can only reconstruct from the genealogy. After all sorts of attempts, I decided simply to present the genealogy and let the reader work out when all these children were being born and from whom. The one thing the emperor didn't write was love letters or little notes!

GM: The genealogy was a very biblical section, I thought.

JS: Yes, it gives the impression of a life of total procreation, going alongside all the political acts. Ironically, his central despair was his own son. So I decided that should be a section of its own, in which the sort of yearning one has for children—I had young children at the time and I think I was very moved by that combination of terror and hope that parents have. One can't believe anything in the world can be worse than something happening to that child. So you watch and—I don't know—you get a piercing sort of caution about the world, I think, and that's what I realized K'ang-hsi was actually writing about. Later, he figured he'd been done in by his son. Psychologically, *he* probably did the boy in by false expectations and endless, endless needling of him. It must have been ghastly. "All the perfect tutors; why can't you shape up?"

GM: In fact, he even educated the boy himself, didn't he?

JS: Yes. You can imagine all those conversations every rebellious teenager has been subjected to in every society. But this poor guy was put under house arrest and eventually killed for it. In a sense, each of those sections slowly grew. There wasn't a plan, exactly.

GM: It emerged from the material?

JS: Yes.

GM: K'ang-hsi appeals to a Western reader by defying some of the expectations one might have about a Chinese emperor. For example, his concern over executions, which he tried very hard to avoid.

JS: Yes, he really did emphasize that concern. But it may suggest too compassionate a picture, because this was a pretty tough fellow.

GM: I wonder if you were consciously editing to try to make him sympathetic?

JS: No. No, not consciously. When he talked about violence, I included it. I tried to make it casual. When he felt somebody ought to be sliced, he sliced him, which to us is a nightmarish idea. But it was one way of capital punishment. Just as today we might hear someone say, "Let's send him to the chair, the bastard," K'ang-hsi's version was, "Let's have him sliced in the marketplace." Then he went on to the next thing. That's why I wanted to get this juxtaposition. That's

159

why I call it a montage, because I jump. I designed the jumps in that case to have a logical sort of flow, to be dramatic movements from episode to episode. We know more about what he did than we do about Ricci or Woman Wang, of course. We have a day-by-day account of all K'ang-hsi's life because of the official histories. If I wanted to, I could say where he was on January 9, 1683. You know, that's the way Chinese history is set up. The emperors were tracked every single day of their lives.

GM: Did you intend in this book to make the Eastern mind accessible to the Western mind? Was that one of your aims?

JS: Yes, I was interested in that, without claiming to understand much about the Eastern mind or the Western mind myself.

GM: How accessible are they? Ricci himself points out how difficult it was to understand the Chinese, even after all those years.

JS: I was particularly drawn to this emperor, not only because of the frankness of those letters and documents, which is very rare, in fact unique, but he was also a person who had in a sense to learn Chinese. It wasn't his native tongue. As a Manchu learning Chinese, he was easy for me as a Westerner learning Chinese to empathize with—first, in that he was trying to learn the language at all, then that he was slowly struggling to be a reasonable scholar and ultimately trying to be a major scholar. I don't think people ever believed he was much of a scholar, but he himself believed he was—that's part of the flattery given an emperor. In that sense, I think that K'ang-hsi was a marginal figure in Chinese civilization and would have been so regarded by scholars around him, the true Chinese

160

Confucians. But they would have been impressed, I think, by his trying.

What I've found in the best Chinese teachers I've had was they liked me for trying to understand their culture even though they knew in their heart that I couldn't and probably would never get anywhere near the bare intuitive understanding of it. I had a couple of very impressive Chinese teachers. The main teacher was called Fang Chao-ying. I went to work with him in Australia in '62. A remarkable scholar and a lovely man.

GM: The *Matteo Ricci* is the most elaborate book you've done and the most difficult to understand. Do you use the memory techniques yourself?

JS: No, because I find it too hard to retain all the attributes of all the images. I think you have to have a very different kind of brain to classify things by it. I cannot use it.

GM: It seems to add another level of memory that makes remembering more difficult.

JS: So the Chinese man said to Ricci, that Chinese governor. He said, "I love your method, but it's too hard to remember." That's such a human comment. And that's what I feel about it. I see it as a kind of baroque structure. I did use it as artifice, which is how it was attacked by contemporaries. People like Francis Bacon were beginning to attack it as supreme and pointless artifice.

GM: We don't know—you don't know—what the images meant to him: the warriors, for example, or the woman from the West. Are they just there, as illustrations of his technique?

JS: They are just there, yes.

161

GM: So it's really your memory palace.

JS: It's my memory palace, yes. Using it again rather as those trigger phrases organized *K'ang-hsi,* I used this to draw everything together about war, or about the idea of the mother and child. You can ask me for a justification, and my only answer is because I chose to.

GM: And the pictures are the same?

JS: That was entirely because it was my personal feeling that the four pictures ending with the mother and child and the four images ending with the mother and child again were not exactly coincidental; there was something more complicated going on, but I didn't know what it was. But for the person sworn to celibacy who had left his mother forever and devoted himself to the mother and child, it seemed to me moderately clear, though I'm certainly no psychologist. In this case, I felt that this would always be the way the thoughts were drawn, and the ultimate goodness, the ultimate vision would be of the mother and child.

GM: In the last chapters of the book, you suggest that the grandmother was the dominant woman in his life.

JS: Yes, I remember I was interested in that. K'ang-hsi, too, had been very, very drawn to his grandmother. Maybe that's because both of my grandmothers died early, I don't know. I would have liked to have known a grandmother. In Proust, too, the grandmother is the overwhelming figure.

GM: You recount Ricci's death in the middle of the book, at the end of the Warrior section.

JS: I was delighted with that. Some reviewers were furious. It made people get angry. I said, "Why shouldn't he die? It's just part of the story. So why not have him die in the middle instead of the end?" One reviewer was particularly cross about it. He said, "This guy doesn't even die at the end, he dies in the middle."

GM: It occurs to me that some of Ricci's earliest memories and experiences are told towards the end of the book.

JS: Yes, that's as you start to unravel the childhood. That's at the coming together of the memories. Well, that wasn't consciously anything except the drawing together of the images. In that book more than any other, the images dictated the sequence because I had two cycles of three and then one juncture. I drew a plan up on the wall. It was one-two-three, one-two-three, and then this one arrow triumphantly meeting where the two streams came together. Then I literally wrote that onto the paper, fairly unplanned, just with boxes, and then I juggled the interconnections between the chapters.

GM: They have been very cleverly tied together. I think of the chapter on Emmaus, and the meal, which is implied in the picture, which you tie in with Ricci's many Chinese meetings, which occurred over meals.

JS: Yes, I liked that. In a sense it's a book, as near as I come, about Christianity, which is maybe a reckless thing to do—certainly, since I'm not a practicing Christian, though I was a very devout Protestant in my late teens and was brought up pretty much knowing the Bible by heart. My school had services every day so I was steeped in the language that was natural to Ricci as well. And without trying to go overboard, I felt close to him in that way.

GM: Of course, he was a product of Catholic education. I wonder how you prepared yourself to treat that.

JS: Well, I read a great many Jesuit works of devotion and talked a lot to Jesuit scholars, who were very generous. I actually gave a symposium on him at a Jesuit research center. I was fairly terrified, but people were very nice. We had a three-hour discussion on some of these theories. But I couldn't be sure I wasn't making grotesque mistakes. I had in a sense to go by instinct.

GM: There proved to be so little about Matteo Ricci personally, compared with a twentieth-century figure, say.

JS: Yes, it's all in the one paragraph in the last chapter, which is when the five senses come together, marking the moments of his life. You know—when he sees, hears, smells, touches, tastes. That to me is the essence of the whole book. That is the biography. Yes, that's this paragraph here, which is each of the five senses, as represented throughout the book through the writing of Saint Ignatius of Loyola:

> He sees the eunuch Ma Tang, suffused with anger, grasp the cross of carved wood to which the bleeding Christ is nailed. He hears the shouts of warning and the howling of the wind as the boat keels over, flinging both him and Joao Barrados into the water of the River Gan. He smells the incense that curls up around his triptych as he places it reverently upon a pagan altar in the luxurious garden temple of Juyung. He tastes the homely food prepared for him by the poor farmers in their country dwelling near Zhadqing. He feels the touch of cheek on cheek as the dying Francesco de Petris throws his arms around his neck.

That was my feeling at the time of how each of the senses would be represented in the biographical mode. Of course, in *The Exercises,* you go through the senses as you confront Christ crucified. Here, he goes through them—or I go through them—as he confronts his own life. I've read Ignatius a lot, especially *The Exercises*—it's about devotion and memory together, and sacrifice. It's a very powerful vision.

GM: I wonder how far one can infer a life from a culture? For example, in the early chapters, you'll sometimes say, "Well, we don't know exactly what Ricci studied, but a typical education would include . . ."

JS: Yes, but inferring a life from a culture is a little dangerous. I felt I could get somewhat in the right direction by doing that, but I wouldn't want to say it could all be pinned down. We don't know; we have nothing specifically about the childhood. We can be sure of the kind of education he had. We know the teachers. We know the curriculum. We know the violence in his hometown. We don't know what he thought of it, but we know how he later wrote of that violence. We're not far off some interconnection. We don't know anything about his sexual life or imaginings. But we know what the standards, what the codes stated by the society were. And we know how emotional he was about his friends and how willing to talk about his emotions, and yet how angry he was and overt when he felt there was sexual misbehavior, so there would be a very complicated moral standard here, which again we can get somewhere toward, as one can by putting Woman Wang in the context of Ch'ing adultery laws. So you get a fairly close context—I'm not trying to get beyond that.

GM: The juxtapositions of Chinese culture and Western culture in this book are fascinating—as in the contrasting attitudes to violence, with Ricci having difficulty discovering the difference.

JS: Yes, and then trying to discover how to apply himself to this difference.

GM: What did you accept as the final insight into the Chinese culture: what you knew from other readings, or what Ricci finally decided?

JS: I tried to stick with him. Some people thought I agreed with him, and that's not necessarily true. I just presented his views. Some people took it as my lack of interest in Buddhism, for example, but that isn't true—I was presenting Ricci's lack of interest and his dismissal of it. Otherwise, one would have had to write a disquisition about Chinese Buddhism, which I was not interested in doing, or competent to do. So that's a clear example. I tried to present how he thought. I did the same with the emperor. The emperor presents his thoughts. In a sense, I tried not to approve or disapprove.

GM: I'd like to ask you about yourself as narrator. In a sense, you are outside the work. You don't interfere and allow the subject to speak, and yet you are so much in it. You are the magician.

JS: This is what interests me most, really. I'm doing the same in the book I just finished. Of course, I am the craftsman and I am the interpreter. What interests me is giving the fullest possible context of the action and then standing back. But of course, you know I'm not really standing back, and I know it. Perhaps it's a search for a voice that has a kind of detachment. That I suppose you could say is a novelistic technique—when the novelist doesn't intervene to say, "Goodness me, I do think that is an improper act!" Of course, an occasional narrator does that, but I'd rather have people mark in the margin: "Yuck!" or "Fancy that!" rather than doing it myself.

GM: How has writing these books affected you? Have they changed your life?

JS: I think each was written in response to a certain moment in my life. I don't know which was changing what. I'm never the same after a book. Some people say I write a lot. I write very slowly, I'm afraid, and with great pains, great difficulty. But my sense of writing is that if I hadn't written the books when I did they wouldn't have been written. They were my only chance to write that way. There's no conceivable way I could write *Woman Wang* again; there's no conceivable way I could write the Ricci book again. As a matter of fact, I told myself that if the manuscripts disappeared at the last minute, as they were going to the publisher, I would make no attempt to recreate them. I would just let them go, because I wouldn't be the same person. Something had been taken out of me. And brought into me. Yes, I think I've been changed profoundly by each book. As I said, each one has been triggered by a very specific period of my life. I don't know if you can age the author by each book. For that reason I never allow any photographs on the jackets. I have no interest in the reader knowing what I look like nor what my age is. I have no interest in that at all.

GM: Can that be because they are such intellectual books? The structures are so intellectually satisfying, and amusing, so witty, that they speak mind to mind.

JS: That's kind of you to say that. That's what I sometimes hope.

GM: Yet they are such emotional books. In spite of your not wanting to be in them, I sense in them a driving creative force, full of feeling.

JS: They are emotional, deeply emotional. They may be substitutes for other things. There's a lot that seeps in to the realm of creative thought which I don't really worry about. I just do it. But it's not easy to do. It's not easy to say one

enjoys it. The words don't seem to fit somehow: "enjoy,"
"easy."

GM: Would you mind telling me what you've just
finished?

JS: Again, it's a kind of reversal of the Ricci book, just as
Woman Wang was a reversal of the emperor book. It's
about one of the first Chinese who ever came to Europe,
and his attempt to cope with European values. In his case,
everything went wrong. He found it terribly hard to cope
with Europe at all. He lived in France, and the French
found it impossible to cope with him, and ended up solving
the problem by shutting him in an insane asylum. So it's a
book about a quest for another culture, to put it bluntly,
ending in madness. But it's got a happy ending, because the
Chinese man gets sprung, but after two-and-a-half years of
incarceration. He ends up back in China again, so the book
ends with him there. It's no attempt to echo the Ricci; it's
just a completely reversed pattern: the man's going around
the earth the other way, he's edging into the languages
backwards, he's confronting the other civilization, he's
Confucian first instead of the other way around, and the
book brings him full circle. He returns to China a sadder
but wiser man—probably sadder and maybe a little bit
wiser. There's no attempt in the book to say that this was a
constructive experience; I just relate.

Here again it's a search for a voice in which to describe
this adventure as it took him around the world into an
unknown continent. Even more perhaps than in the other
books, I'm just trying to watch this unravel. It's a very
chronological book. I've dated every episode in the man's
journey. I present it more in the form of a dated chronicle,
in a series of episodes in maybe one- or two-page accounts.
Like the *K'ang-hsi*, I wrote it mostly in the present. I
switch, but most writing I do in the present. I find it satisfy-

ing to write in the present. But it's very hard, much harder to do.

GM: Do you enjoy rereading your work?

JS: I usually don't reread my things, or if I do, I have to wait several years. I do the proofs and galleys, and then this book arrives and I just look at it. And shake my head.

GM: What are you reading?

JS: The opening passage of *Emperor of China,* which I haven't looked at for years: "There are some wild geese that live far beyond the northern frontiers, a little-known species that leaves the north just before the first frost, and flies down into China. The border guards use their coming as a sign that the first frost is on the way. I had some caught, and caged in the Ch'ang-ch'un Garden at the water's edge, so they could drink or peck up food at will. In springtime, near them, the crested white ducks play upon the water, and in other cages are peacock and pheasant, quail and parrot, and baby cranes no larger than your fist. Deer lie on the slopes—fallow deer and roebuck—and if you poke them with a stick they stand and stare."
Hmm. It's lovely. Good stuff.

Conversation with

Elisabeth Young-Bruehl

When I met with Jonathan Spence, he asked me if I intended to interview the biographer of "that excellent biography" of Hannah Arendt. I knew exactly the one he meant, because I remembered reading a long review of it on the front page of *The New York Times Book Review* section several years before. The photographs of the beautiful young Hannah had caught my attention, and after reading the review, I decided to read the biography, *For Love of the World*. But I still hadn't done it.

Spence's comment prompted me to read the biography at last. As I did, I reveled in the dazzling intellectual company of both subject and author. The day I finished the book, I contacted Elisabeth Young-Bruehl. She responded with an invitation to meet her in New Haven, at the Atticus Cafe. Every week, she said, she came down from Middletown, where she was teaching in the philosophy department at Wesleyan, to attend a seminar at Yale. I waited in the combined bakery-eatery-bookshop, enjoying the smell of fresh bread and coffee.

A little past eleven, an intense-looking woman with graying hair, cut short, hurried in and came right up to me. She was dressed in a loose shirt, jeans, and clogs. "I'm Elisabeth Young-Bruehl," she said. "Are you looking for me?" She gave me a firm handshake.

We talked our way through coffee, lunch, and more coffee—three-hours' worth of far-reaching discussion about Young-Bruehl's biographies (she was just finishing a second biography, of Anna Freud, which has since appeared), and about biography in general.

Gail Mandell: Do you mind if I tape our conversation?

Elisabeth Young-Bruehl: When people ask me for interviews or ask if they can tape them, I feel that it would be unfair of me to say "no." I spend my life asking people to do both for me.

GM: Everyone I've spoken with has been very generous. I guess that may be because they too depend on the generosity of others!

EYB: Everybody in the contemporary biography business knows that if people don't deal openly and generously with each other, nothing happens. I have a long history of people making my books for me.

GM: Making your books for you?—oh, I see, because of what they've told you.

EYB: Yes. They provide me with something. In the case of the Anna Freud biography that I've just finished, I had minimal material to construct Anna Freud's childhood. Now, when your method is psychobiographical and your subject is a child analyst who is herself the child of the founder of psychoanalysis, to have minimal material on the childhood is a disaster. Then I went to London and I met this wonderful woman who had been Anna Freud's companion and caretaker in the last year and a half of her life, when she was very ill. This woman was a German-Jewish émigré—like all the people that I spend my time talking to!—who had been farsighted enough, understanding enough of what she was doing to keep a journal of the entire year and a half she spent with Anna Freud, when Anna Freud was speaking German a lot of the time, off in her childhood and reminiscing about things. Manna Friedmann had a record of all that; I could not believe it when I read it. A miracle.

Things like that are fortuitous. But nothing happens unless you can get to people and win their trust. To do that, you've got to know enough about what you're doing so that they can be sure you're not going to abuse them, or that you're not some cheap scandalmonger.

GM: Are you educated in psychology—is that why you're interested in psychobiography?

EYB: No. I had my higher education, as they call it, in literature. I studied creative writing at Sarah Lawrence College, with Muriel Rukeyser, a poet, who taught there. But I was a college dropout in the 1960s, and after I did that for a while, I went back to school at the New School for Social Research, and ended up at its Graduate Faculty, where I studied with Hannah Arendt and did a Ph.D. in philosophy, primarily in political philosophy. Slowly over the years since then I've moved in the direction of psychology, and particularly psychoanalysis.

GM: When did your interest in biography begin? Was it with the biography of Hannah Arendt, or before?

EYB: I never had the slightest idea that I would write a biography, but after Hannah Arendt's death there was a memorial service for her at Bard College, where she's buried. Actually, the interment of her ashes had to wait until the spring because the ground was frozen. At any rate, gathered at this occasion were a lot of Hannah Arendt's old friends, and one of them said, "Someone must write a biography." I nodded. They started discussing the materials that were available, and who should do this and that kind of thing. Then one of them turned to me and said, "Why don't you do it?" I said, "Oh, no," but then I thought about it a while later.

At first I didn't think I would do a biography. I thought that I would go around and interview all these people and their similar numbers elsewhere and do a kind of oral history of her life. I don't think that at that time I had ever read a biography of anybody. I had no idea what a biography was. So I set out to do that, and soon I was so hooked that I thought, "Well, I might as well try and do the whole thing." I had such incredible material! That's one of the things that's addictive about the biography business—you start on a small scale and unearth things, and the story grows and grows and grows. There's more and more to tell, and each time you find something, it leads you to something else. You get caught up in the detective work, which becomes very fascinating.

I think that everybody now writes psychobiography perforce—no way to avoid it. Some people like me do it full-scale, like this Anna Freud biography—but everybody does it to some extent.

GM: What exactly do you mean by "psychobiography"?

EYB: Simply something psychologically oriented and guided by psychological theory.

GM: I ask, because your biography of Hannah Arendt didn't strike me as obviously psychoanalytic.

EYB: No, the Hannah Arendt one really isn't; the Anna Freud one is. It's very, very different. I sometimes can't even remember that I wrote the Hannah Arendt book. It was so long ago, so different.

GM: I believe you called Hannah Arendt's biography a "philosophical biography"—

EYB: I did, and that's what I thought I was doing, but I don't think I succeeded too well.

GM: What did you mean by that?

EYB: I wanted to be able to understand her way of thinking from one book to the next and one idea to the next: a life of the mind. And I did that, more or less successfully, but "philosophical" was the wrong word to choose there. It's got a connotation of professional or academic philosophy about it, and that is not what I produced. I really should have said, "This is a life of the mind biography," or something more like that. In retrospect, I also think that in many respects the biography of Hannah Arendt was a psychologically unastute biography. I know more now. I see now that there are places where I missed opportunities for psychological understanding.

GM: To tell you the truth, I was surprised that I liked your biography of Hannah Arendt as much as I did, because I've never read any of her writings.

EYB: You don't need to have read them. I considered that a challenge—to make the life accessible to those who weren't familiar with the work. That's one reason I was drawn to Anna Freud, too. It seems to me that nobody, not even the psychoanalysts who bow down at the feet of her reputation, have made any good general statements about her work. They know this essay, this book, this other thing, but not the work as a whole, or why it evolved from this point to another point. It was my privilege to do that, to pull it all together and write what in effect is a long, sustained introduction to her work. That's the way I conceived both books. The work of both women is difficult—but in different ways. Anna Freud's writing style is pellucid—unbelievably clear—but that clarity masks an incredible complexity of thought.

GM: You never met Anna Freud, did you? But you did of course know Hannah Arendt.

EYB: Yes, Hannah Arendt was my teacher.

GM: Was it easier working on someone you knew, or not?

EYB: It's hard to compare. In many ways, I think I came to know Anna Freud better than I knew Hannah Arendt, although I actually spent a lot of time with Hannah Arendt. But that's because of the kind of material that was available. Hannah Arendt was one of the most decidedly unself-reflective people. You can see it in the biography. There's seldom a quotation from her letters or the work in which she explicitly reveals herself, and says, "I felt this." Her comments are all directed at the world: "I think this about this thing over here." There are very few explicitly autobiographical, self-reflective statements.

GM: Of course, there were her poems.

EYB: Yes, and I spent a lot of time on those poems because they were, I thought, the most revelatory of the documents that I had. Although there is not any directly autobiographical work in Anna Freud's published writings, her letters are the most introspective and revealing letters I've ever seen, because she thought about herself quite psycho-analytically. You have psychoanalytic self-reflection—self-analysis, really. It's constant. It's ideal. If I were reading my book, I would be astonished by the depth and lucidity of her self-insight. If you have somebody who understands herself as well as that, you should set up the book to let that self-understanding come forth as clearly as possible—just organize it.

GM: In a way, it sounds as though you think of yourself as a mouthpiece through which the subject speaks.

EYB: Yes. I organize the person's self-understanding and present it as it evolves over time. I relate it to the work as it evolves over time, and also to the friendships and the love affairs and the marriages or whatever as they emerge over time.

GM: Do the differences in the two biographies perhaps reflect your idea that the way you tell a life has to reflect the life somehow—has to be appropriate to the way the life was lived?

EYB: Absolutely.

GM: And just how do you know what's appropriate? How do you make that judgment?

EYB: You work on it for a while. You gather the material and see what you've got before you can make any decision about what kind of book to write. That's one of the things that's very complicated—it's a technical complication. You have to wait a long time before you know what's appropriate, and the character has to emerge to you from whatever materials you've got before you can really decide what kind of book it will be. That's why I call the initial technical decisions in biography writing the "organization of the files"—that is, how you get your material organized in some kind of way.

Usually this involves a rough chronological map, just so you will be able to file things in such a way that you can get back to them and so you can see what I call the "morphology" of the life emerging. It'll have certain turning points in it, certain points of great density, certain points that lack density, certain places where the material clusters, certain places where the material is bare. You have to know that landscape from the beginning to the end of the life before you can decide what kind of life it is that you'll write. Or even where to begin.

Most biographies have a chronological frame to them, but that's just a modus vivendi with most good biographies. I think one of the clearest signs of a bad biography is that it relies too much on its frame. It's too beholden to its frame. The frame can't tell you much about the way the person experienced his or her life—that's an entirely different thing. For example, I think one of the most important things to know about people is the periods of their lives which they can't remember, or which meant nothing to them, which are like blanks in their memories. Those are often the ones that you need to be most interested in, even if you find them most underrepresented in the material.

GM: How do you identify and then uncover those?

EYB: You have to set up your materials so that the period emerges as best it can from what you've got, and then ask as many questions about it as possible. Sometimes you'll get it to emerge and sometimes you won't. Once you get the material ordered initially, you'll find these blank periods in the documentation, and you have to make a maximal effort to fill them. Other places that are richer take care of themselves. But those bare ones often will be the really revelatory ones. Often they contain a secret—if not a conscious, sometimes an unconscious one. Sometimes you can do something with that and sometimes you can't, but at least you know where to set your sights.

The other thing that I think is important is that you have to fit the biography to the subject, and to me that means primarily to the subject's character. But also you have to fit the biography to the subject's way of writing, if yours is a subject who produces texts: to the kind of thing that they've produced, to the content of it, and the style, and to the method of its production. These will be your clues to the way the person's mind worked.

GM: In other words, as you the biographer tell the life, you want the reader not just to experience *your* way of putting things together, but—

EYB: I want the person to be inside the mind of the person who is making the texts so that the reader knows as clearly as the biographer can possibly reconstruct it why the subject went from this text to that one, why they went over here, and then sidetracked and did this one, why the style of this one emerged into the style of that one, what the continuity between them was—I want my reader to be inside the literary production as much as possible. So I have to know as much as I can about how those books were made—how they were put together, where they were written, all that sort of thing. It's not a commentary; that's an entirely different thing. It's about the manufacture, about the creative process, whatever you want to call it.

Obviously, you know enough from reading around that people have different ideas about whether and to what degree you should make your biographical work visible. Some people feel that you should master the material, compose your frame, and keep your distance. They're doing

178

something like portrait painting there; then they put a frame of their own making around the subject. Others foreground themselves—as the biographer—so that you feel them in the texts making judgments. The biographer steps right into the biography. You feel the biographer making judgments, putting material together, telling the story. I am of completely the opposite school of thought—that you should not appear in the biography at all, that the reader should feel as though no one wrote it, and that they should simply feel that the story is completely compatible with the subject's life. Told, if not the way they would have told it themselves, at least in a way that they would recognize. You even have to feel that the subject would recognize this life intimately as his or her own. That's my primary criterion.

GM: But one you can't test out.

EYB: No, you can't—thank God!

GM: Your approach seems to demand absolute identification of the biographer with the subject.

EYB: It requires a very great degree of identification, but also the ability to step back from that a little bit. It's a very tricky psychological process. I can only write biographies of people with whom I feel identified and about whom I feel very positive. I have to feel really strongly that this life is worth telling—that it's the kind of life that I really want the people reading this book to know about. That conviction has to be very strong. The danger in this sort of approach is lack of critical distance.

Several who reviewed my Hannah Arendt book accused me of hagiography, of being uncritical, and I can understand that. In fact, I agree with the criticism that it was uncritical. I never set out to criticize. Here again, there are different theories of how to do things. I didn't have any theory at all

179

when I started, but as I did things, that's what I decided I wanted to do—to take the perspective of my subject. I decided the *Anna Freud* would be, if anything, more that way. I didn't correct myself at all from one book to the other. If I have a capacity to identify with people in this kind of way, why should I work against it?

I feel that my approach is particularly good for someone who did not write an autobiography or any kind of memoir or leave any sense explicitly in the writing of how he or she thought introspectively. Then the life is not available on the subject's terms and so you have a perfect path to recreate it that way. I would never do that for somebody who was a prolific writer of memoirs or autobiographies. Anaïs Nin would be the sort of subject with whom I would never use this approach.

GM: Why not?

EYB: Because she wrote her memoirs constantly. Then your job as a biographer would be to try to make a comparison between that vision of her life and the facts as you could construct them.

GM: When you describe what you are doing with someone like Anna Freud, it sounds as though you're compensating for what they didn't do—that you're taking up where they left off.

EYB: Private persons just are not memoiristic. In fact, I think the best subjects of biography—but this is my particular bias—are the ones who intensely guarded their privacy. They kept it within, and so you can find it; but those people who spread it out for the general public in memoirs—I think they dilute their private lives. And they also introduce all kinds of complexity, because people will relate to them by what they know about them from the books they have written about themselves, so the access of people to them is mediated by their own autobiographical circle of wagons. To get to the real person is a terrific project—you have to penetrate the personal myth.

You can tell I'm never going to write my autobiography, can't you?

GM: Looks like you'll have to reproduce yourself if you want somebody to write your biography!

I'm interested when you imply you don't judge, because when you wrote about remembering in an article published in *The Partisan Review* a few years ago, you said that the real task of the biographer is to memorialize.

EYB: That's the way I think of it.

GM: And you go on to talk about how remembering is judging—how the two go together. I'm curious about that, because if you are judging by the act of remembering, how can you divorce yourself from judgment?

EYB: This is a kind of philosophical point. If I can, I'll explain. I think there are two very different kinds of concepts of judgment. One involves true standards or ethical standards, or whatever standards you want, which you apply to the subject. This kind of judgment is very often present in biographies, and I find it unedifying. I wouldn't treat my best friend that way, and neither would you. Say you were having this conversation about your friend's decision to divorce her husband. I doubt you would say, "Divorce is terrible!" In other words, you wouldn't take an "a priori" set of criteria and apply it to the subject. People don't relate to each other this way if they care for each other. If they do care, they have a long discussion about the decision: "What do you have in mind? What brought you to that?" You reconstruct with the person the whole process of coming to that decision, and then you're there with them, making the decision, seeing how it was done. It's a process of judgment about what all of the factors coming into decisions mean—that's the whole memorialization process. That's an entirely different kind of judgment from closed, moralistic or external standards—so-called universal standards—that you apply to everybody. I wouldn't live that way, and I certainly wouldn't write a book that way. But some people do.

GM: That reminds me of the difference Carol Gilligan sees in the sort of principled judgments typically thought of as male and what she calls female ways of judging.

EYB: I don't think that's a gender-specific difference; she does. Lots of people speak in a different voice; some of them are male.

The kind of thing I'm talking about can easily be considered wishy-washiness, where all that's understood is excused. In my own mind, I say to these moralistic biographers, "What right have you to judge? I mean, you have your best reasons for thinking what went on, but you don't know." There's a kind of arrogance in that approach.

GM: Does that explain what you meant when you wrote of the Arendt biography that you wanted to provide a context for a life? That yours was not a critical biography but a contextual one?

EYB: Yes. It's contextual. If my readers want to make a judgment, let them. I give them all the information I have about what was going on at any given moment.

GM: That seems to fit in, too, with what you say about the power storytelling can have when the story is told in such a way that the conclusions haven't been drawn for the reader.

EYB: Yes. Walter Benjamin says that's what makes a good story, and I agree. That is what a story is. That's what distinguishes a story from a fable. With a fable, you get the moral; it's the tail that wags the dog. I just tell the story. If somebody else then wants to draw a moral, that's their privilege—but I usually don't approve in the slightest.

One of the things I find interesting about the reviews of my Hannah Arendt book is that, because I didn't write a fable and draw a moral, many of the reviewers did. They jumped in with their reviews and came to some conclusions about this part or that part of Arendt's life, or the whole.

GM: Did writing the biography of Hannah Arendt influence your idea of biography?

EYB: Yes, both positively and negatively. I was very satisfied with that book as a way of studying the evolution of a work, but very unsatisfied with it as a psychological study. The Hannah Arendt book is reflected in the Anna Freud book in the technique of showing the evolving self through the work, but there is added to the Anna Freud book a much deeper level of psychological study. I learned a lot about how to organize and research a book, which I carried over totally from the Hannah Arendt book to the Anna Freud. That made it possible for me to write the Anna Freud book much more quickly, because I knew how to make a filing system. My students always think I'm very funny when I say that a book is only as good as the filing system, but it's true.

I have a very intricate filing system. I started out the Anna Freud book with three filing systems which had evolved out of the previous book. One is a chronological file based on a notebook that has a page or sometimes two for every year of Anna Freud's life, so that I can tell you where she was at any given moment. That's like the index to everything else. Then there's a vertical chronological file that goes along with it, with files in it of major events—major things that happened, like "school years," and everything I can find out relating to that goes into that file. Then I have a people file—a file for every major person in her life. In Anna Freud's life, that's a cast of thousands. That's a great big file. Some folders have only a few things in them, but others are huge, where I have copies of the major works of her major friends. Then there's a thematic file. As I work along and particular things seem to me to be crucial themes in her life and work, I make a file for that, and sometimes some of the same material from the other files I'll copy and put in that file.

Periodically, I'll read through those folders again, to keep at the top of my mind the main threads of thematic networking that are going to connect the narrative. Then, as I write the book, I create the fourth file, a chapter file, as I get the material broken down into units. Sometimes the chapters change as the book goes. Slowly, as I write the book, I move the material from the other files over into the chapter folders, so that by the time I've finished, the first set of three files has shrunken considerably. They're still there, but a lot of material from them has moved over into the chapter folders, and is there to build up the book with.

I find this system enormously efficient. I always have the material right where I need it. Sometimes I put notes in the chapter folders that say, "See such and such," and refer back to one of the other files. But basically the book is writing itself in those chapter folders, and I break it down into pieces of the chapter as I get that organized in my mind. Also, when it comes to the dreary business of doing all the notes, the documents are all right there in the chapter folders—you don't have to search back through the other files to find things.

I'm talking about four big file drawers of material to make a four-hundred-page book out of, so that's an enormous amount of material, and if you don't have a filing system to be able to lay hands on it, you're lost. It would take you forever to write a book.

GM: Do you use a word processor to write the book?

EYB: Yes, I write on the computer, but I don't keep notes on it. I do all that by hand, because I have to be able to have it in my hands. When I'm getting ready to write a chapter, I take all the relevant material out of the chapter folder. I have a huge desk that has nothing on it except a big light, and I lay all that material out on it and rearrange the pieces of paper as I see the story unfolding. I have my computer at another desk, and I take the pieces that seem to be the beginning of the chapter over there and write that out and think about it, and slowly build it up. But I like to be able to see what the whole of the material for that chapter is, and then I can imagine the narrative thread much more easily—I just reorganize the pieces of paper. I make outlines from having all the material visually in front of me.

The trouble with the computer is you have to flip back and forth. You lose the kind of overview that you literally get if you lay it all out. The computer is a temporal catalog, and you must go back and forth, but the spatial thing is much truer to the way a life is laid out. It's much truer to visualize it in space rather than time, because then the themes come out at you. In time, you're too reliant on the chronology. Let's say you're dealing with ten or fifteen years of a person's life in one chapter. If you relied too heavily on the framing there, you would fail to see that something had happened here and something had happened over there, and these are the things that really go together because they are thematically related. Dwight Macdonald once made the only true statement about composition that I ever heard: "Put all the things on the same topic in the same place." If you're too tied to the chronology, you'll never do it. You have to find a way to realize that, for example, two trips, one made in 1945 and one made in 1950, have something in them that is a third topic; the dates you give in passing. The important connection has to emerge from the material. You can't get it by just turning the pages of your day-by-day chronology of a life, any more than you could if you were reading a person's appointment calendar.

GM: Which stage do you enjoy most when you are writing a biography?

EYB: The last one I described, when I have everything all laid out in front of me and I start making the connections. I hate getting all the research done. I hate all the libraries. I hate all the facts. I only like it when it begins to fall together. Then it's really composition, a creative and exciting thing. All the rest of it is drudgery.

GM: How long did you spend gathering material for the Anna Freud book?

EYB: About a year and a half.

GM: That's fast. Were you teaching at the same time?

EYB: No. I left my job for two years. I wanted to do it without interruptions. I was also under pressure to do it because only a few of Anna Freud's friends were still alive. I had to go interview them very quickly, or I wouldn't have them available at all. Of ten older people that I interviewed, six have since died.

GM: You talked about how you came to write the biography of Hannah Arendt. How did the idea of doing the book on Anna Freud first occur to you?

EYB: It didn't occur to me at all. The literary executor asked me to write the book.

GM: Did it take you a while to warm to the idea?

EYB: I had always admired her work very much, what little of it I knew. Then, too, I was terribly excited by the prospect of a full-scale, interesting biography of a lesbian. I thought, "Terrific! This will be great!" Well, she wasn't a lesbian. I was very disappointed, because the rumor was that she was a lesbian, and I thought, "Wonderful! Here will be a story of monumental achievement by a homosexual woman." I fell right on my face. I had to control my disappointment in her. I had to understand as intricately as I could why she would live fifty years with another woman, and in a quite platonic "Boston marriage," as they call it.

GM: And you did come to understand that?

EYB: I did my best. I respect it, and I have no trouble with it now that I've finally worked it all through. But it really was a disappointment. I had never been able to feel much sympathy for chastity. It always seemed to me somehow a screen. But now I've developed a considerable sympathy for it. A colleague and I had a funny discussion about this just the other day. She read the third chapter, in which I try to understand the "asceticism," as I call it, of Anna Freud. She said, "As I get older, I'm much more appreciative of chastity." And I had exactly the same reaction. I thought, it was a good thing I didn't try to write this book when I was a young woman, when I was much less understanding of the importance in a certain sense of—the word is a strange one here, "husbanding" our resources—saving our sexual resources for other things and developing modes of sublimation. I think it's something that a young person would be hard-pressed to appreciate unless she were like that herself. So I had a new task: to make a person who had no sexual life at all "sexy," as they say in the jargon of the day—that is, to be really interesting. How was I going to get Mr. and Ms. General Reader to be fascinated by a woman who had no sex life at all?

But that wasn't the challenge I set out with. I was going to make them appreciate a lesbian, and that would be a real triumph for most people. I had given a good deal of thought to various strategies: I was going to assume homophobia on the part of my readers—and then work with it and win them over. I spent a lot of time thinking about that before I came to the conclusion that she wasn't a lesbian at all.

You do have to anticipate your readers' resistances, and deal with them as best you can. And that's one good reason for knowing your own resistances very well, because readers will often have the same ones. But you have to write with great confidence that your way of dealing with the resistances is going to overcome them, and just go on. If you're all the time wondering whether you've overcome them, you'll write defensively.

So I had a new task for myself. There are some things here that I think my readers will find difficult, like the fact that Sigmund Freud analyzed his own daughter. What it must be to be psychoanalyzed by your own father!

GM: Sounds like incest.

EYB: Sounds like incest. I expect my reader to be repelled. I'm repelled, though not as much as I think most of my readers will be. The strategy I use is to tell the story of the psychoanalysis three different times through three different sets of material. The first time, I tell it through some poems that Anna Freud wrote when she was in analysis, so I get people used to the idea in a literary-critical context, which I think is easier for most people than a strictly

188

psychoanalytic one. Then I tell it again in psychoanalytic terms. Then I tell it again in terms of its consequences for her theory and her work. I'm sure that most of my readers will never realize they've been through this three separate times because it's all woven together very intricately. But each one of those tellings is designed to hit a particular set of resistances that I anticipated from my readers and worked with.

GM: Who wanted the analysis? He? She?

EYB: Both. They didn't trust anybody else. Also, she was a particular kind of a case, and he knew it. He had been involved with her case as it unfolded, long before she ever got to his couch. They were going to have to deal with that anyway. I use this as an occasion to teach a great deal about psychoanalytic technique and the problems of what is called "transference."

GM: Another attraction of biography—all you learn as you read about a life.

EYB: Whole worlds.

GM: That reminds me. You've written briefly about why you subtitled the Hannah Arendt book: *For Love of the World.*

EYB: Some people find that sentimental.

GM: You explain that you see biography as a product of love of the world, as an act for the world, not out of any particular love of or friendship for the subject.

EYB: Although that may be where it starts—what one feels initially.

GM: I'd like you to explain your ideas about that a bit more fully. Do you feel you owe it to the world to write the biography of certain people? Do certain lives demand to be told?

EYB: Yes. Some lives need to be told.

GM: Because others need to hear them or you need to tell them?

EYB: Both. I think you write most deeply out of your need to tell it, but I don't know that you'd be brought to it if you didn't also feel that other people needed to hear it. In the preface to the Arendt book, I quoted that passage of hers from *In a Dark Time,* the collection of biographical vignettes that she wrote, that says something to the effect that, "In dark times we have a right to expect some illumination, and some lives cast a light upon the world." I feel very much that that's true. But there are very few lives like that, and if there is one and you know about it, and that light has not made its way as a light into the world, then you have a real teaching opportunity.

People have always needed their lives of the saint, or their lives of great Greeks and Romans for pedagogical purposes. Biography in the twentieth century has taken over for people from all kinds of backgrounds—religious backgrounds, ethnic backgrounds—this task of telling exemplary lives. It's a cultural task. But biographies don't serve any particular ethnicities or religions, like the Catholic lives of the saints. Biography is a genre that should cut across all that. In that sense, biography is cosmopolitan. It's concerned with a life in the world, not some particular world—although the life may be lived in a particular world. But it should go beyond that particular world, like a kind of cultural ambassadorship.

I find it a very important task. People need examples—stories of how people live their lives—particularly in difficult times but also in ordinary times. And where else will they get them? They certainly won't get them from the journalists, even though we make docudramas and God only knows what else of everything that happens. But that's all here today and gone tomorrow, even though sometimes they're very well done. A book is something you read, put on the shelf, it's with you for a long time, you can go back to it, it has resonance to it, it's not packed into an hour on the TV or a page in a magazine. People don't learn anything from what they read in *People* magazine, except to be *au courant* with the latest something or other.

GM: Something that interested me about the biography that Hannah Arendt wrote of Rahel Varnhagen was the time she spent in the middle of the book going into the woman's dream life. That sounds like a fascinating innovation.

EYB: It was very unusual at the time. But she doesn't really do it very well.

GM: It is not a good biography?

EYB: Oh, I think it's an excellent biography. But it's very particular. It was courageous to pay such attention to the woman's psychological life—it's just that Hannah Arendt didn't know very much at that time. So it was an adventurous thing for her. Later she did the portraits in the volume called *In a Dark Time,* which were much more sophisticated. She had lived a while, and, even though those are not explicitly psychological portraits at all, there's an extraordinary astuteness about people in them, about ways of being in the world that shows you how youthful an endeavor the Rahel Varnhagen book was—adventurous and brilliant, but youthful.

GM: Did you find yourself imitating Hannah Arendt's biographical style?

EYB: No, not really. What I did was to imitate her later styles, from her later books, but not that little book. I used much more the style of the *In a Dark Time* portraits and her *The Human Condition.* Even down to the details, I imitated it. For example, there is her "on the other hand" habit. She shows you one view and then the alternative view, the other side of the question. You feel the mobility of mind when she lays it out this way, then comes to a full stop and lays it out this other way. She does this all the time. Very Germanic. But it actually has Greek roots. In ancient Greek, you put the particle *men* at the beginning of the sentence and it means "on the one hand," and the particle *de* means "on the other hand." My book is full of these kinds of locutions: lay it out this way, then lay it out that way. Conceptual maps of things—this is very Arendtian, and I wanted my reader to get used to it, to experience it, so I self-consciously constructed it. It was a way to introduce my reader to her thought without the reader knowing it was happening.

I do the same thing in the Anna Freud book. Anna Freud's theoretical statements are usually very succinct, immediately followed by an illustrative case. She'll say something and then immediately bring out a little boy of six who does this and that and the other kind of thing. Just when you think, "I don't understand," suddenly on walks this child, who does a particular bit of behavior; then it's totally clear to you what she meant. My book is very often constructed with a dense theoretical passage, and then zip! in the next paragraph I go into a part of her life which shows you exactly what it means—and this is her style. In fact, if you're really into Anna Freud's work—and I think this is often the way a person feels after they read her work—you can hardly remember her theoretical statements at all, but the case vignettes are plastered on your mind.

This is part of my concept of what biography is, that you get that kind of intimacy and familiarity with a person's way of thinking and doing things so that it becomes a kind of second nature to you. What you do is write Hannah Arendt's life as you would have intellectually experienced Hannah Arendt doing it, being it, living it, had you known her.

What really fascinates me—and I may have created this; it may not be there—is that both Hannah Arendt and Anna Freud were in many ways extremely conservative as thinkers. Hannah Arendt recaptured Greek categories from Aristotle for the present day, and Anna Freud was terrifically dedicated to the preservation of psychoanalytic theory as her father had laid it down, and she was tremendously conservative in this. But both of them were also revolutionary, boundary-breaking, unconventional people and thinkers. The more I contemplate this, the more it seems to me—an outrageous generalization!—that this is really the combination of character and intellectual traits that makes for a great work of genius. This radical conservatism and this radical unconventionality are often quite complementary. Both women seem to have had a profound sense that revolution, unless it has an impulse to lay down conservative foundations, will easily fall into the destructive maxim of revolutions, that the end justifies the means, and self-destruct. To counter that, you need an argument which will always come in some form from tradition.

GM: Did you feel your attitude to Hannah Arendt or Anna Freud changing as you worked your way through their biographies? Especially to Hannah Arendt, whom you knew?

EYB: I was amazed to find out how little I actually knew about Hannah Arendt. Also, how little everybody else knew. One of the things that was most interesting was finding those poems of hers. When I went to Vienna to interview her first husband, I asked about those poems, some of which she had written during the time of their marriage and some before, when she was with Heidegger. "Poems?" he said. "She wrote poems?" That was such a clear indication of how much she kept to herself. Then I found that motif again and again and again. She kept secrets. I only found three people in her acquaintance who knew that her father had died of syphilis, and only a few people knew about the Heidegger affair.

Now, that's an incredibly important thing to know about a person—how close-mouthed they are about themselves. How unconfessional. Many people of course blather on all the time about themselves—they make a life out of confession. There's some fascinating psychoanalytic literature on the need, the compulsion to confess. Of course, confessing endlessly is a way of telling nothing. So there are two ways to tell nothing—one is to keep a secret and the other is to seem to keep no secrets whatsoever. Entirely different structures of personality are involved in these.

No, I had no idea that Hannah Arendt was such a secret-keeper. I could have guessed, but I just never thought about it. You learn so much about what you don't know about people. It's like a huge jigsaw puzzle with thousands of pieces, of which you saw only five pieces and thought that was the whole puzzle. Makes you realize how little you know about anybody. That sounds like the most elementary thing in the world and I feel like something of an idiot to say it, but we come to our realizations in different ways. Maybe I was rather slow, but after spending five years of reconstructing a life, I was deeply impressed by how little I knew about the lives of anybody I knew—or loved for that matter. I think that's one of the things that adds to the great allure of psychoanalysis. The knowledge that one can have of another person's life is deeper and more thorough looking this way. And if you use it right, if you don't misuse it and exploit it and you're not instrumental about it, you can know more lovingly this way than with any other approach to a human being. Because the things about a person that

194

may seem quite incomprehensible at first don't look the same if you work at them long enough with this kind of method. That is, if the other person yields himself or herself to some extent to you.

For example, I came across a passage in which Anna Freud, as an old woman, wrote to a friend of hers about two memories from her childhood of times when her father was "tender" to her. That was her word. She told two stories. Then she said that this tenderness was what she wanted for the rest of her life, more than anything. I thought about this tenderness. What did she mean? What was it that she wanted? Finally, I said to myself, "Well, I don't know *exactly* what she wanted, but tenderness is what she should get from her biographer." Only that kind of attitude toward her, only that one that she most desired, was the one to which she would reveal herself. So if I were going to write about her, then I should love her that way. That's the frame of mind in which I would hear her. I took a chance at the end of the book, and after the part about her death, I wrote a final paragraph, which is an image that captures that feeling—it is a tender image of her. I want my readers to go away from the book with that image sealed on their memories. I want the reader to say, "Oh, that's the way it was with her. I see." But before I came across that passage about her father—as I say, I'm a slow learner—this would not have occurred to me. It's a funny thing: I might know this about the real people I love, as opposed to the ones I've imagined, and know it about my own need to love, but I somehow hadn't translated it into my work.

Then I had this wonderful experience. I went to the New York Academy of Medicine to lecture before the Association for Psychoanalytic Medicine, or some high-flown title like that. I read them the part of the book that deals with Anna Freud's analysis with her father. Afterwards a woman came up to me, shook my hand and said, "I don't think I've ever heard a more tender presentation." I nearly fell over. I embraced her and said, "Thank you very much. You have no idea what you've said." Full circuit. For me it was a miraculous thing, in a way, that she should choose exactly that word, exactly that feeling. It was particularly important for me—this is confessional, by the way—because a lot of people who know me know me as very tough. Very tough. And I can be very tough. But that's not all I can be. Parts of this book are very tough, too—the ones that deal with controversies, with the fighting within the psychoanalytic movement: it's presented in a tough, clear, rational way. But the other strand, the basso continuo, is the one I really wanted and worked for.

GM: And that was partly because you felt that was what she would have wanted.

EYB: That's what she wanted—spent all her life looking for. I mean, she got it from people, too. She got it to a certain extent from her father, from her companion, and from a couple of other people. Somehow she got it from the woman who took care of her in the last year of her life, the woman who kept the journal. She needed it; she got it. But there's also justice that she should get it from somebody who takes the responsibility to tell her life.

In the same way, I ask myself, what did Hannah Arendt need? What I thought she needed at the time was impartiality. But no, she wouldn't have wanted tenderness. Her strongest desire was always to be understood. She had a passion to understand—she always said that. What she needed, to a degree, was a passion to understand her. She always looked for people who would really engage her in intellectual conversation. It's not for nothing in her later work that she's always talking about thinking as an interior dialogue. She was always looking for people to have a thinking conversation with. Anna Freud was not looking for that at all.

GM: Challenging for you to try to give to both women what they needed.

EYB: That's the theory of biography I've been trying to describe to you. That's where the biographer gives something to the subject and doesn't demand something for herself. In public. Gets something enormous in the privacy of her own life, but doesn't put it in the book. What's in the book is what the biographer gives. I would say, "I am at your humble service"—that's the attitude of the biographer in the book. But as I say, that's a very particular kind of approach to biography. You ought to interview somebody at the other pole, too.

GM: When you wrote about Hannah Arendt's biography of Rahel Varnhagen, you titled that section "Biography as Autobiography"—

EYB: Yes, though I don't think she really knew that. I mean, I think she was to some degree self-conscious about how connected she was to this Rahel character, but I don't think that she was as aware as she might have been of how much she needed Rahel's story for self-understanding.

GM: Is it true of you also, that for you biography is autobiography?

EYB: Very definitely so.

GM: But you're not going to say how?

EYB: Mnnn.

GM: Strange then that you would think of yourself as distanced from your work—

EYB: But I don't think of myself as distanced from my work. Not at all. There's a difference between what the work means to me, and what I put there for the reader to read. Just because I say that I don't want to be in the book—present to the reader all the time—that doesn't mean that I'm not there in the book. It's just that the reader shouldn't know it.

GM: Only you should know it?

EYB: I should know it. I should know it as thoroughly as possible. To the extent to which I don't know it, the book will fail because I'll be working without the kind of self-reflection that it takes to know the difference between me and the person and how my judgments, submerged as they are in the text, are influencing it. If I don't know my own blind spots fairly well, I'll just reproduce them in the book. But that self-knowledge on the biographer's part is no business of the reader.

GM: So that's what you meant when you wrote the biographer must be an "achieved self"?

EYB: Yes. If my reader read either the Hannah Arendt book or the Anna Freud book and was preoccupied with the question, "What kind of person is this Elisabeth Young-Bruehl?" I would have failed totally. I don't want them even to ask. I want them to be caught up completely in the question, "Who was Hannah Arendt?" or "Who was Anna Freud?" That doesn't mean that I'm not asking all the time who I am, but I don't need the medium of this book. I work it out in the process of writing the book, but not in the text of the book. It's prior. That's one reason why with me every book that I've ever written, and certainly these two biographies, goes through multiple drafts, and one of the things that happens is that self-knowledge is brought to bear on each draft, and as it changes, I get myself more and more out of the book.

GM: It sounds like a therapeutic process for you.

EYB: It is—certainly. That's one reason I have to take a character I really admire, because they operate for me as a kind of ego-ideal or a character-ideal. Both of these women I've written about, and it's no accident this is the case, are strong, unabashedly intellectual, self-confident, rangy, uninhibited thinkers, exactly as I myself wish to be. Watching them do it is a very important part of my self-formation. I play off against it all the time, and I find that very, very valuable. A very valuable way to grow up. But you don't want that growing up process to be there in the book. At least, I don't. Now, people have very different views about that, and it's important to realize that this that I'm telling you is just one way.

I had an experience that illustrates these differences. A reviewer of my book for *Feminist Studies* complained that my voice was not there in the book; that I didn't allow myself to ask what she thought were the really important questions about Hannah Arendt, like, "What was it like for Hannah Arendt to be a woman?" I didn't ask this sufficiently for her. In contrast, she praised a biography of Simone de Beauvoir, which includes a long letter that the biographer wrote to Simone de Beauvoir. I can't remember whether she actually sent this letter to de Beauvoir. At any rate, she felt it necessary in the middle of the writing of the book to engage in self-catharsis by writing a letter to Simone de Beauvoir about the complexities of the biography, and how Simone de Beauvoir reminds her of her mother. She put her whole personal life and struggle right there in the book.

Now this is the opposite end of the spectrum from my idea of how to write a biography. But it's a school of thought, and it's very common in biographies of women by women, particularly when the woman chosen as the subject of the biography is playing an ego-ideal kind of role in the writer's life. To put that struggle right there in the book and make it part of the appropriation of woman's biography is something!

But you have to recognize it as part of a spectrum of opinion about the biographer's role in the biography. The reviewer has her view of what that should be—and with precedent. I mean, James Boswell is forever right there in Samuel Johnson's biography saying what he had for breakfast, and it's a brilliant book. But Boswell is not always reflecting on himself in the same kind of way—the "What did Dr. Johnson mean to me?" kind of way. I think it's very difficult for biographers at either pole to understand or to appreciate the other extreme.

GM: Would you say there are other biographers working now who try to do the same thing you do, or do you feel alone as a biographer?

EYB: Interestingly enough, I think a majority of biographies of women by women go in the opposite direction from mine—at least the ones that I've read recently, the ones where the biographer is right there telling you how much the subject means to her. This is very, very common, because it's part of a new feminist trend of discovery of women's problems in our "foremothers," as they call them. So I find that most of the biographies that I now admire are by men. That's a little too bad, but these things have their fashions. You have to recognize the limits of your own psychic constitution and your preferences about these things. I would be hopeless in this other mode.

GM: Are your biographies of these two women different in any way *because* they were women and you are a woman?

EYB: Very much so. But let me give you a little information first, and then generalize. Hannah Arendt married her second husband, who was considerably older than herself, and very self-consciously decided never to have children. She had her work, and she lived in times that would have made having children very, very difficult. In her childbearing years, she was in exile with no security whatsoever. This is a life in which that particular feminine role of child bearer and mother is self-consciously refused.

When she died at the age of eighty-six—almost eighty-seven—Anna Freud was a virgin who had never had a love affair, never even had a serious courtship. Her companion of fifty years was a very interesting woman named Dorothy Tiffany Burlingham, an American who was also a psychoanalyst. Dorothy Burlingham had four children, so she and Anna Freud had Dorothy Burlingham's four children—Dorothy was separated from her husband, who later died. So here's another very unconventional family life.

A lot of feminist biography these days is very interested in contemporary questions about how a woman will balance, for example, her literary life and her mothering life—how she'll get all that together. Although it's a very interesting problem, it's of no interest to me, personally, so I wouldn't care to take it up. But I'm very interested in these lives which are much closer to my own in terms of the kinds of decisions that are made and the way the life is organized, and the foregrounding in the life of work. So everybody will look across the spectrum of things and find certain woman-to-woman, woman biographer-to-woman subject questions interesting, and proceed accordingly. A lot of women write about women who identified with the women's movement in its earlier incarnations; there are many biographies of Mary Wollstonecraft, for example. But neither of my women had the slightest tolerance for feminism or for the women's movement. This is something that I disagree with personally—I gladly identify myself as a feminist—but that's not my primary concern, and I turn to the way in which my women criticized feminist concerns with great interest because I think there's something to be learned from it for feminism. I think some of the most important criticism of feminism comes from women who refuse it. I take that as a particular topic of interest, but for many identified feminists, that's nothing but a bane. So these questions set themselves up differently.

Still, the woman question is always going to be there in many different forms in a woman's biography of a woman. Both my women were Jewish, specifically German-Jewish and Austrian-Jewish. I'm not Jewish, but I find certain Jewish cultural and family traits very compatible. However, they're not compatible with certain other kinds of interests that women would have in writing about women. You must find your way in the territory of these things. But it does make a great difference that you are a woman writing about a woman in one way or another.

You can take the same topic from another angle. The only biographical work on Anna Freud had been done by men, and they were not even slightly interested in the questions that were of primary concern to me. On Anna Freud there are two existing biographies, one by a German and one by an Englishman. I find them useless in the extreme, because they don't even raise as questions the things that I take to be most important in Anna Freud's life. That's mostly because I'm a woman with a particular take on things. I doubt it even passed through their minds to ask these questions. The first chapter of my Anna Freud biography is devoted to an intricate portrait of the Freud family and the relationships between the siblings of this family of six children. If you grow up in a family of six children, this is a crucial thing. That's a lot of children—and you're the littlest. And there are three adults: your father, your mother, and your mother's sister, and nursemaids as well. There were eleven people living in this house. It makes all the difference in the world that a child lives in the midst of eleven people and is the tiniest. That's an utterly formative experience. I spend the first chapter laying it out in intricate detail. These other biographies just say, "She's the littlest."

GM: Of course unless she wrote about it, it must be hard to reconstruct what that meant to her.

EYB: You have to think about it. First of all, you have to ask the question, then you go get all the tiny pieces of information that are here and there and weave them into the story. They're there, but if it's not a question for you—"What was it like to be the littlest in a household of eleven?"—you don't even look.

GM: It must be interesting to read a biography of your subject by another person. Were there any others of Hannah Arendt?

EYB: No, mine was the first book that even said a word about her biography. There was nothing to go on. On the other hand, it was a totally open field. Because many people connected with her were still alive, there were questions of discretion: how to tell the story in such a way that it did not compromise the privacy of people who were still living. Contemporary biography is a mine field of discretionary judgments, and that's one of the most difficult things about it.

GM: Do you think you'll go on writing biographies?

EYB: I don't have another person in mind. But when I get a couple of things I've been working on off my plate, I'm going to write an interpretive essay on the work of Marguerite Yourcenar. Yourcenar's early work has never been translated into English, nor has her autobiography.

I'm assembling all the material, and I'd like to read it and see. She died a few years ago, and apparently the estate is with her publisher, Gallimard; I've asked my literary agent to find out what the story is. But if Yourcenar turns out to be as interesting as I think that she might be, I may start with an essay and then move on. I'd have to go very cautiously. She appeals to me though, in part because she was trained in the classics as I was. Her first book was a little book on the early Greek poet Pindar.

GM: How do you make a decision—read the things a person has written, and read about the person to the point where—?

EYB: Where you understand whether your minds are compatible. People set out on tasks that they think will be right for them, and then they give them up. This can happen, for example, if someone experienced in literary biography takes up a subject who did not produce literary texts—a performer, a musician. So I would try to make a choice well before I got launched, and stop with an essay if things didn't look promising.

GM: I can imagine how difficult it must be to interpret a personality without texts. I do recall, though, that you quoted Hannah Arendt as saying that she wondered whether literary people were fit subjects for biography.

EYB: Yes—her very limited view!

GM: She thought people of action were the ones who should have their lives told.

EYB: That's her particular view of biography, with which I disagree.

GM: Do you have any thoughts on what distinguishes literary biography from other types?

EYB: Some people think—and I don't; I disagree with this—that you can interpret literary works or, say, performances, or political actions as if they could all be read and interpreted in similar kinds of ways—like in psychoanalytic theory you would say that a person's writings and their behavior and their dreams and their slips of the tongue all reveal the subject's psychic configuration and impulses. That's fine for psychoanalytic theory, but if you think that a person's actions can be read like a text or that a text can be read like actions, you can get enormously confused, because you read out of account all the different kinds of constraints that surround people acting with other people. They do what the situation allows them to do. For example, if you are looking at a person's ideas and actions in a political realm, you can read them like a text, but you have to read them with an acute sensitivity to a context that is very difficult to recreate. Every significant political act could be a book, because of the number of threads woven into it. A literary person will certainly be enormously complex, but the person and the texts can be seen and studied by themselves. That's a different kind of reconstruction. Everything flows in from the past, but you don't have to create a complete context as you do with political actions. The moment of a political act is quite exteriorized, and you have to get all the participants painted. I frankly think it's impossible.

I totally disagree with Hannah Arendt and think it's almost impossible to write a good biography of that sort because it's too complicated.

GM: Maybe she was thinking only of events and their consequences, which could be told like a story.

EYB: But if you want to know what really went on, you'll never find out. It's too complicated. You may be able to find out pieces. The other thing that defies your management is that there's a different cast of characters, a different technique for telling it. On the other hand, a text is there. You can start with that and finish with that.

GM: Perhaps because there is something static about a text, and something so dynamic about actions and decisions?

EYB: A literary biography has anchors in it. There will always be unanswered questions about it, but they won't be the same kind of unanswered questions as a political narrative raises. You can put a piece of that text in front of the reader and say, "Here, this is what I'm talking about."

GM: That gives the biographer a certain authority, too, I suppose.

EYB: And allows the reader of the book to share. If I put a piece of Hannah Arendt's poetry there, and I translate it for you, already you're getting it mediated because you're getting it in English and not in German. I put it there for you; you read it; you read what I write about it; you say, "I agree," or "No, I think this or that," but at least there it is and you can read my opinion and you can have your opinion, and you can think about it. But if I'm telling you the story of certain events, unless you go to the archives and call up all the newspaper reports, you have to take my word for it. The whole thing is reconstructed by me. And then we're not sharing it. So it's a different relationship between the reader and the writer of the book. A lot of people think that when you're writing about political history, you're writing about facts, but you're not.

GM: It's an interpretation?

EYB: An interpretation. But the reader doesn't always know it. Whereas in literary biography, you know it. You know this person is reconstructing events. You feel it all the time: "And here's this, it was written then." You know it's the biographer's task to tell you what happened, and you feel the biographer doing that. Very often in political biography, the illusion is created that you were there, this is what happened, and that wonderful sharing that goes on between the reader and the writer of the literary biography is absent, because the reader doesn't have anything to share. You can say to yourself if you read a biography of, say, John Kennedy, "Did it happen that way? Somehow I remember . . . ," but you're calling on your memory of twenty-five years ago. The power of the political biographer to recreate events is enormous because there isn't any check. That's why I don't like it.

GM: It sounds like you don't trust it when you read it.

EYB: I never do, at least not when the writers try to over-sell their version of the events. They so seldom throw up their hands and say, "Who knows?" They say, "It must have been," or "Undoubtedly such and such." I was enormously impressed to find at the end of Barbara Tuchman's *Guns of August,* which is really quite a marvelous book, full of the historical recreation of events, at which she's very good, a statement to the effect that if the historian ever says to you, "It must have been," don't trust her or him. But they say it all the time!

I'm not a pettifogger about detail. I'm very often content in my own books to try to sweep over things. But I always let my reader know—there's some sort of signal: "This is an approximation." I put a little statement at the beginning of the Hannah Arendt book indicating that when I found different versions of events, I made an amalgam and cut loose threads away. I tell my reader at the beginning of the book: "This is a construction. Some people say this, and some people say that." There's a paragraph in the Anna Freud book explaining how difficult it is to go through this territory, because of the different opinions about it and the number of lies that have been published in various places. My reader is reminded from the beginning that biography is a patchwork. "There will be gaps, and I'll try to tell you where they are." But some people are committed, and most political biographers are, to the seamless story.

GM: Maybe that's changing now, with a new awareness of history as narrative.

EYB: Yes, I think it is changing. Thank goodness. The methodological self-consciousness is a bit higher now than it used to be. And social history has done wonders for political history, because everyone knows that no social situation could be compassed in a volume. Now, if some political historian comes along and ignores contexts completely, then you're very well aware.

GM: Do you think that there has to be something of the creative writer in every biographer?

EYB: I write fiction as well as biography, and a lot of biographers do, I think. They live very much on the margins of scholarship. The biographer must first of all be a storyteller.
I just finished reading Peter Gay's biography of Freud. That's a very capable book—a real historian's book—all the details are marshalled. He's very present in his book as the biographer. He's in there saying, "Freud did this, and I think that about it," only he doesn't usually enter through the first

person singular and say, "I think this." He says, "One would agree," or "One would disagree." But even though this book is encyclopedic, very thorough, there's not a story. There are no narrative lines or moments that really move this book from one part to another. There's no suspense. There's no point in the book at which you say, "God, and then what happened?" or "What do you suppose they're going to do?" None of that, which you get if the facts serve the story. Gay's is a particular kind of biography; it's a historian's biography, where all the details matter, where there's not a great deal of selection in the details—everything is there. There's no story to compel certain of those details to come forward and certain others to recede, or even disappear. So it's very capable in its way, and it exemplifies a certain kind of approach. You're not inside Freud, where you see the world as he did, moving from one project to another. There's a very good account of the evolution of Freud's work, but it's just the evolution of his work—the biographer is not inside the subject, moving from this idea to this next one.

GM: I'm curious about your response to the current widespread interest in biography. What do you make of it, and of biography today?

EYB: Biography is a genre whose modern origins are in the 1920s. Of course it has its big antecedents, say in the eighteenth century, and it has its Plutarch, but it's basically a twentieth-century phenomenon. It is a particular cultural effervescence, and to understand why this should be so and why the fascination should be so is one of the most interesting questions to ask yourself as you think about this genre as a genre.

For me, this was one of the big challenges of writing Anna Freud's biography. The presence in our century of psychoanalysis is obviously one of the things that has changed the whole climate of opinion concerning biography. As Auden liked to say, Freud *is* a whole climate of opinion. The kinds of things that you inquire about in a person's life or things that you need to know to understand them are dramatically different than they ever have been before. And on a mass scale. So that makes it a peculiarly interesting challenge to write the biography of a child of the founder of this particular cultural phenomenon. It's a very interesting set of questions: What difference did it make to be raised in the household of a man who thought like that; to be literally a child of psychoanalysis? It makes for a real opportunity for reflection on what I said very explicitly in the introduction to this biography of Anna Freud: this was a life lived psychoanalytically. The question is, what does that mean? And the rest of the book is really to tell you what that means. What is it like to live your life that way? To take psychoanalysis not as a theory but as a whole way of life?

One of the things that I think makes the biography-writing business so complicated today is that people who review biographies and even write about them don't have any ideas about these things. There's no critical perspective. I mean, when you read a good review of poetry, you can get from the review and from quotations a pretty good sense of what this poetry is like, but people who review biographies generally content themselves with retelling the story of the life, saying it is well done or ill done, and you have no idea what the strategy for the biography is. There's no cultivated readership for biography, because people are only reading for the life story. If you asked most people, "Well, what kinds of things make a good biography?" you would draw a blank. They would have nothing really to say, nothing about whether that tale was well or ill told—the craft of it.

Biography is not a very neat business. It evolves with the times, and it learns from evolving fictional techniques. I think you can sometimes tell from a good biographer's work what kind of fiction he or she enjoys. For myself, I enjoy psychological acuity, and the thing I really like, which is very rare, is the broad-stroked psychological but also historically, politically, and socially acute epic novel of the sort Toni Morrison writes in *Beloved*.

I learned a great deal from Toni Morrison's *Beloved*. I thought about what it would be like to construct a biography in which there were certain elements of character or events contributing to the subject's development that didn't come clear till the end of the book. Both you the reader and other people in the book would come close to understanding, but wouldn't. Then, at the end of the book, as with *Beloved*, you would sock yourself in the forehead and say, "Oh, yes, that's what it is!" Only a particular kind of life could be told this way, one that would have something in it that the subject herself was out of touch with, but which might actually have evolved into conscious understanding, past the barriers of consciousness that the subject herself had set up. The biographer would have to wait until the end of the life to reveal what the subject finally understood. Given the right life, one that demanded such a technique, it would make a fantastic biography.

Once you leave the narrow confines of conventional biography, there are many ways to tell a life. But the models for these kinds of adventures are fictional. Any good biographer explores those far reaches of biography constantly. It may have no direct effect on your work at all, but it does keep you from over-reliance on the chronological frame and all the kinds of things that make a biography flat as a pancake—what I call the "laundry list" biography, in which every speck of information you came across in the course of researching the book has to be in the biography because you've got it—you know, what William Faulkner ate for lunch.

I think the rarest thing to find in the biography of a person who writes texts is a really good integration of the life and work, where you don't alternate from the life to the work and back again. I think it's done fairly successfully in my biography of Hannah Arendt. But the reason for that is no great talent of mine; the reason is that the political events of her life carry the life into the works and back again; you can tell the story of the life and the works through the mediation of political events, which the work reflects. It's very different with someone who was closed off—who, say, lived in wildest Vermont with a typewriter and everything coming out of her head.

I think that the integration of life and work in my Anna Freud book is also very good. But once again I had a third ground to do the mediation for me, and that was the development of psychoanalytic theory. It plays the same role that political events play in the Hannah Arendt book—it moves you back and forth from the life to the work. The first half of the Anna Freud book is a double biography, the biography of Anna Freud and Sigmund Freud, and the development of his theory mediates both their relationship and the emergence of her first psychoanalytic work. The latter part of the book was more difficult to do: he dies, she goes off on her own, and the relationship between her life and his theory is much less intimate. In the first half of the book it was easy to keep this alternation going, but in the latter part of the book it was very tough to keep my reader from feeling that the book had lost its cohesion.

A lot of people who write biographies, particularly people who come at it from literary criticism, where they're used to analyzing or deconstructing a text, just stop the story to give you two pages of analysis. One way to tell good biographers from bad is to note whether or not they have brought that problem of how to relate the life to the work, to the foreground of their minds. That's a very good rule of thumb for measuring the success of the endeavor. There are lots of ways to proceed, depending on what the life is, what the work is, what's dictated by the materials that you've got.

You know, I think it's a good thing you're going around to talk to a lot of biographers. It's a good way to learn about the genre. I think you'll be struck again and again by the diversity of personalities who bring themselves to this art. It's not a genre that attracts a particular type of person, like particular types of fiction attract particular types of people. I went once to a biography seminar at New York University, at the Institute for the Humanities. As I listened to the biographers, I thought: "If you brought a stranger in to listen to these people and played 'What's My Line?', you would be baffled. They totally defy your expectations." But biographers are a very interesting group of people.

Works Cited

General:

Oates, Stephen B. *Biography as High Adventure: Life Writers on Their Art.* Amherst: University of Massachusetts Press, 1986.

Woolf, Virginia. *Collected Essays,* Volume IV. New York: Harcourt, Brace and World, 1925, reprinted 1967.

Of the Biographers:

Paul Mariani

A Commentary on the Complete Poems of Gerard Manley Hopkins. Ithaca: Cornell University Press, 1970.

Crossing Cocytus: Poems. New York: Grove Press, 1982.

Dream Song: The Life of John Berryman. New York: William Morrow, 1990.

Prime Mover: Poems. New York: Grove Press, 1985.

Timing Devices: Poems. Boston: David R. Godine, 1979.

A Usable Past: Essays on Modern and Contemporary

Poetry. Amherst: University of Massachusetts Press, 1984.

William Carlos Williams: A New World Naked. New York: McGraw-Hill, 1981.

William Carlos Williams: The Poet and His Critics. Chicago: American Library Association, 1975.

Edwin McClellan

Woman in the Crested Kimono: The Life of Shibue Io and Her Family Drawn from Mori Ōgai's "Shibue Chūsai. New Haven and London: Yale University Press, 1985.

Michael Mott

Counting the Grasses: Poems. Tallahassee, Florida: Anhinga Press, 1980.

The Seven Mountains of Thomas Merton. Boston: Houghton Mifflin, 1984.

Arnold Rampersad

The Art and Imagination of W. E. B. Du Bois. Cambridge, Massachusetts: Harvard University Press, 1976.

The Life of Langston Hughes. New York and Oxford: Oxford University Press, 1986. Volume I: *1902–1941: I Too Sing America;* Volume II: *I Dream a World.*

Phyllis Rose

Jazz Cleopatra: Josephine Baker in Her Time. New York: Doubleday, 1989.

Parallel Lives: Five Victorian Marriages. New York: Knopf, 1983.

Woman of Letters: A Life of Virginia Woolf. New York: Harcourt Brace Jovanovich, 1978.

Writing of Women: Essays in a Renaissance. Middletown, Connecticut: Wesleyan University Press, 1985.

Jonathan Spence

The Death of Woman Wang. New York: Viking, 1978.

The Emperor of China: Self-Portrait of K'ang-hsi. New York: Knopf, 1974.

The Memory Palace of Matteo Ricci. New York: Viking, 1984.

The Question of Hu. New York: Knopf, 1988.

Elisabeth Young-Bruehl

Anna Freud: A Biography. New York: Summit Books, 1988.

Hannah Arendt: For Love of the World. New Haven and London: Yale University Press, 1982.

Mind and the Body Politic. New York: Routledge, 1989.